1969 U.S. YEARBOOK

ISBN: 9781790563081

This book gives a fascinating and informative insight into life in the United States in 1969. It includes everything from the most popular music of the year to the cost of a buying a new house. Additionally, there are chapters covering people in high office, the best-selling films of the year and all the main news and events. Want to know who won the World Series or which U.S. personalities were born in 1969? All this and much more awaits you within.

© Liberty Eagle Publishing Ltd. 2018
All Rights Reserved

INDEX

	Page
Calendar	4
People In High Office	5
U.S. News & Events	9
Worldwide News & Events	19
Births - U.S. Personalities	23
Notable American Deaths	30
Top 10 Singles	33
Top 5 Films	39
Sporting Winners	55
Cost Of Living	64
Comic Strips	77

FIRST EDITION

1969

January						
S	M	T	W	T	F	S
			1	2	3	4
5	6	7	8	9	10	11
12	13	14	15	16	17	18
19	20	21	22	23	24	25
26	27	28	29	30	31	

○:3 ◐:11 ●:17 ◑:25

February						
S	M	T	W	T	F	S
						1
2	3	4	5	6	7	8
9	10	11	12	13	14	15
16	17	18	19	20	21	22
23	24	25	26	27	28	

○:2 ◐:9 ●:16 ◑:23

March						
S	M	T	W	T	F	S
						1
2	3	4	5	6	7	8
9	10	11	12	13	14	15
16	17	18	19	20	21	22
23	24	25	26	27	28	29
30	31					

○:4 ◐:11 ●:17 ◑:25

April						
S	M	T	W	T	F	S
		1	2	3	4	5
6	7	8	9	10	11	12
13	14	15	16	17	18	19
20	21	22	23	24	25	26
27	28	29	30			

○:2 ◐:9 ●:16 ◑:24

May						
S	M	T	W	T	F	S
				1	2	3
4	5	6	7	8	9	10
11	12	13	14	15	16	17
18	19	20	21	22	23	24
25	26	27	28	29	30	31

○:2 ◐:8 ●:16 ◑:24 ○:31

June						
S	M	T	W	T	F	S
1	2	3	4	5	6	7
8	9	10	11	12	13	14
15	16	17	18	19	20	21
22	23	24	25	26	27	28
29	30					

◐:6 ●:14 ◑:22 ○:29

July						
S	M	T	W	T	F	S
		1	2	3	4	5
6	7	8	9	10	11	12
13	14	15	16	17	18	19
20	21	22	23	24	25	26
27	28	29	30	31		

◐:6 ●:14 ◑:22 ○:28

August						
S	M	T	W	T	F	S
					1	2
3	4	5	6	7	8	9
10	11	12	13	14	15	16
17	18	19	20	21	22	23
24	25	26	27	28	29	30
31						

◐:4 ●:13 ◑:20 ○:27

September						
S	M	T	W	T	F	S
	1	2	3	4	5	6
7	8	9	10	11	12	13
14	15	16	17	18	19	20
21	22	23	24	25	26	27
28	29	30				

◐:3 ●:11 ◑:18 ○:25

October						
S	M	T	W	T	F	S
			1	2	3	4
5	6	7	8	9	10	11
12	13	14	15	16	17	18
19	20	21	22	23	24	25
26	27	28	29	30	31	

◐:3 ●:11 ◑:18 ○:25

November						
S	M	T	W	T	F	S
						1
2	3	4	5	6	7	8
9	10	11	12	13	14	15
16	17	18	19	20	21	22
23	24	25	26	27	28	29
30						

◐:2 ●:9 ◑:16 ○:23

December						
S	M	T	W	T	F	S
	1	2	3	4	5	6
7	8	9	10	11	12	13
14	15	16	17	18	19	20
21	22	23	24	25	26	27
28	29	30	31			

◐:1 ●:9 ◑:15 ○:23 ◐:31

PEOPLE IN HIGH OFFICE

President Lyndon B. Johnson
November 22, 1963 - January 20, 1969
Democratic Party

President Richard Nixon
January 20, 1969 - August 9, 1974
Republican Party

Born August 27, 1908, Johnson assumed the Presidency following the assassination of President John F. Kennedy on November 22, 1963. Johnson is one of only four people who have served in all four federal elected positions. He died January 22, 1973.

Born January 9, 1913, Nixon served the 37th President of the United States until 1974 when he resigned from office, the only U.S. president to do so. He had previously served as the 36th Vice President from 1953 to 1961. He died April 22, 1994.

90th & 91st United States Congress

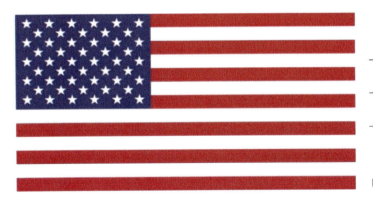

Vice President
Hubert Humphrey / Spiro Agnew
Chief Justice
Earl Warren / Warren E. Burger
Speaker of the House
John McCormack
Senate Majority Leader
Mike Mansfield

U.S. Flag - 50 stars (1960-Present)

United Kingdom

Monarch
Queen Elizabeth II
February 6, 1952 - Present

Prime Minister
Harold Wilson
October 16, 1964 - June 19, 1970

New Zealand

Soviet Union

Ireland

Prime Minister
Keith Holyoake
December 12, 1960 -
February 7, 1972

Communist Party Leader
Leonid Brezhnev
October 14, 1964 -
November 10, 1982

Taoiseach
Jack Lynch
November 10, 1966 -
March 14, 1973

	Country	Leader
	Australia	Prime Minister John Gorton (1968-1971)
	Brazil	Presidents Artur da Costa e Silva (1967-1969) Military Junta (1969) Emílio Garrastazú Médici (1969-1974)
	Canada	Prime Minister Pierre Trudeau (1968-1979)
	China	Communist Party Leader Mao Zedong (1935-1976)
	Cuba	President Osvaldo Dorticós Torrado (1959-1976)
	France	Presidents Charles de Gaulle (1959-1969) Alain Poher (1969) Georges Pompidou (1969-1974)
	India	Prime Minister Indira Gandhi (1966-1977)
	Israel	Prime Ministers Levi Eshkol (1963-1969) Yigal Allon (1969) Golda Meir (1969-1974)

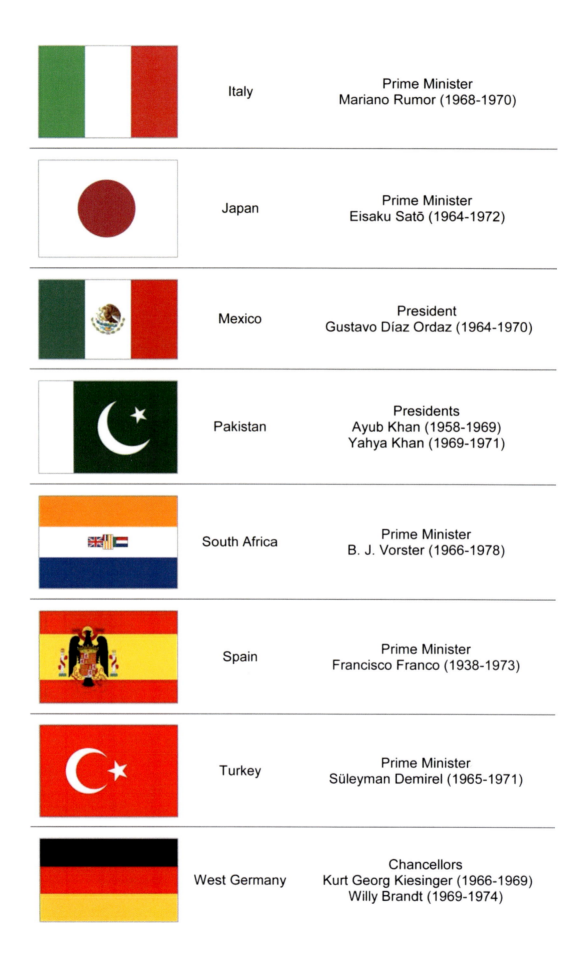

	Italy	Prime Minister Mariano Rumor (1968-1970)
	Japan	Prime Minister Eisaku Satō (1964-1972)
	Mexico	President Gustavo Díaz Ordaz (1964-1970)
	Pakistan	Presidents Ayub Khan (1958-1969) Yahya Khan (1969-1971)
	South Africa	Prime Minister B. J. Vorster (1966-1978)
	Spain	Prime Minister Francisco Franco (1938-1973)
	Turkey	Prime Minister Süleyman Demirel (1965-1971)
	West Germany	Chancellors Kurt Georg Kiesinger (1966-1969) Willy Brandt (1969-1974)

U.S. NEWS & EVENTS

JAN

1 — The Ohio State Buckeyes defeat the USC Trojans 27-16 in the Rose Bowl to win the national title for the 1968 season. Rex Kern, the Ohio State quarterback, is named Most Outstanding Player in the bowl.

9 — In Washington, D.C., an exhibition of Winslow Homer's (1836-1910) graphic art goes on display at the National Collection of Fine Arts (now the National Museum of American Art). *Fun Fact: Homer is recognized as one of the leading figures in American art, known especially for his dramatic marine scenes and realistic depictions of American life.*

January 12 - Super Bowl III: The American Football League's New York Jets defeat the heavily favored Baltimore Colts of the National Football League 16-7. The game, played at the Orange Bowl in Miami, Florida, is regarded as one of the greatest upsets in American football history. Jets quarterback Joe Namath was named as the Super Bowl's most valuable player, despite not throwing a touchdown pass in the game or any passes at all in the fourth quarter.

13 — Elvis Presley steps into American Sound Studios in Memphis, Tennessee, and records his landmark comeback sessions for the albums, From Elvis In Memphis, and Back In Memphis. The sessions yield the popular and critically acclaimed singles Suspicious Minds, In The Ghetto, and Kentucky Rain.

14 — A fire and a series of explosions aboard aircraft carrier USS Enterprise near Hawaii kills 28 and injures 314. The total cost of repairs, including replacing 15 destroyed aircraft, is over $126 million.

16 — Ten paintings, including a Rembrandt, are defaced at the Metropolitan Museum of Art in an apparent protest against the museum's 'Harlem On My Mind' exhibition.

18 — United Airlines Flight 266 from Los Angeles International Airport crashes into Santa Monica Bay four minutes after take-off; all 38 people on board are killed.

20 — Richard Nixon is sworn in as the 37th President of the United States.

28 — A blowout on Union Oil's Platform A in the Dos Cuadras Offshore Oil Field spills 80,000 to 100,000 barrels of crude oil into a channel, and onto the beaches, of Santa Barbara County in Southern California. The spill has an immediate and significant impact on marine life in the Channel, killing an estimated 3,500 sea birds, as well as marine animals such as dolphins, elephant seals, and sea lions. The public outrage engendered by the spill, which receives prominent media coverage across the United States, results in numerous pieces of environmental legislation. The incident also inspires Wisconsin Senator Gaylord Nelson to organize the first Earth Day on April 20, 1970.

28 — Heisman Trophy-winning running back O.J. Simpson, from USC, is the first overall pick in the NFL Draft by the Buffalo Bills.

FEB

8	After 147 years the last issue of The Saturday Evening Post, in its original form, hits stands (the magazine is revived as a quarterly publication in 1971). *Fun Fact: The Saturday Evening Post was first published on August 4, 1821 and quickly grew to become the most widely circulated weekly magazine in America.*
9	The Boeing 747 'jumbo jet' makes its maiden flight after taking off from the Boeing airfield in Everett, Washington. Test pilots Jack Waddell and Brien Wygle are at the controls with Jess Wallick at the flight engineers station.
17	Aquanaut Berry L. Cannon dies of carbon dioxide poisoning while attempting to repair SEALAB III (an experimental underwater habitat developed by the U.S. Navy) off San Clemente Island, California.
17	Four hundred MLB players boycott spring training over owners' refusal to increase their pension-fund contributions along with television broadcast revenues.
24	The 26th Golden Globe Awards are held honoring the best in film and television for 1968. The winners include Peter O'Toole, Joanne Woodward and the film The Lion In Winter.
24	Tinker v. Des Moines Independent Community School District: The Supreme Court makes a landmark decision that defines the constitutional rights of students in public schools. The Tinker test is still used by courts today to determine whether a school's disciplinary actions violate students' First Amendment rights.

MAR

2	Phil Esposito becomes the first NHL player to score 100 points in a season in a 4-0 win over the Pittsburgh Penguins. He finishes the season with 126 points.
3	In a Los Angeles court Jordanian citizen Sirhan Sirhan admits that he shot and mortally wounded Senator Robert F. Kennedy on June 5, 1968.
3	NASA launches Apollo 9 carrying crew members James McDivitt (Commander), David Scott (Command Module Pilot), and Rusty Schweickart (Lunar Module Pilot). They spend ten days in low Earth orbit testing several aspects critical to accomplishing a successful moon landing - testing includes the Lunar Module engines, backpack life support systems, navigation systems and docking manoeuvres.
10	In Memphis, Tennessee, James Earl Ray pleads guilty to assassinating Martin Luther King Jr., and is sentenced to 99 years in the State Penitentiary. Ray dies in prison on April 23, 1998, at the age of 70.
12	The 11th Annual Grammy Awards are held recognizing the accomplishments of musicians during 1968. The winners include Dionne Warwick and Jose Feliciano; Simon & Garfunkel's 'Mrs. Robinson' wins the record of the year.
28	Former U.S. General and President, Dwight D. Eisenhower, dies after a long illness in the Walter Reed Army Medical Center, Washington, D.C.

APR

2	The Milwaukee Bucks sign Lew Alcindor (aka Kareem Abdul-Jabbar) who would go on to play 20 seasons in the NBA and become one of its greatest ever players. *Fun Facts: Abdul-Jabbar was a record six-time NBA Most Valuable Player (MVP), a record 19-time NBA All-Star, a 15-time All-NBA selection, and an 11-time NBA All-Defensive Team member. A member of six NBA championship teams as a player and two as an assistant coach, he was twice was voted NBA Finals MVP.*
4	Heart surgeon Dr. Denton Cooley implants the first temporary artificial heart in to the chest of Haskell Karp, 47, of Skokie, Illinois. Karp survives for 65 hours after the operation.

April 14 - The 41st Academy Awards, honoring movies released in 1968, are presented at the Dorothy Chandler Pavilion, Los Angeles. It is the first ceremony to be staged there and the first time since the 11th Academy Awards that there was no host. The year is notable for the first - and so far, only - tie for Best Actress, with Katharine Hepburn (in The Lion in Winter) and Barbra Streisand (in Funny Girl) sharing the award. The Best Actor Award went to Cliff Robertson in Charly, and the movie Oliver was the winner the Academy Award for Best Picture.

28 | The 4th Academy of Country Music Awards is held at The Palladium, Los Angeles, honoring the industry's accomplishments during the previous year. Hosted by Dick Clark, the winners include Glen Campbell and Cathie Taylor.

MAY

10	The 'Zip to Zap' riot: As a result of an article which had originally appeared in North Dakota State University's The Spectrum newspaper, between 2000 and 3000 people descend upon the small town of Zap, nearly 300 miles from the NDSU campus. Revelers drink copious quantities of alcohol and as the small country town's resources become depleted the amiable mood turns ugly. Zap's residents ask the visitors to leave, some comply, but others stay behind and the event escalates into a full-fledged riot. The National Guard is called in and the crowd disperses leaving damage estimated to be in excess of $25,000.
10	U.S. troops in Vietnam begin an attack on Hill 937 (the Battle of Hamburger Hill) against the forces of the People's Army of Vietnam (PAVN) - it is eventually taken on May 20, through a direct assault, which causes extensive casualties to the PAVN forces. The hill, having no real military significance, is abandoned on June 5 causing much controversy within both in the American military and public.
14	Last Chevrolet Corvair is built at Willow Run Assembly near Ypsilanti, Michigan. *Fun Facts: The Chevrolet Corvair was the only American designed mass-produced passenger car to use a rear mounted air-cooled engine; a total of 1,786,243 vehicles were produced between 1960 and 1969.*
15	A teenager known as 'Robert R.' dies in St. Louis, Missouri, of a baffling medical condition. In 1984 it is identified as the first confirmed case of HIV/AIDS in North America.
18	NASA's Apollo 10 space mission is launched with a 3-man crew consisting of Thomas P. Stafford (Commander), John W. Young (Command Module Pilot), and Eugene A. Cernan (Lunar Module Pilot). The flight is a test run for the first Moon landing and successfully tests all aspects of a lunar landing, except the actual landing. The crew conduct a lunar orbit and lunar descent to about 9 miles from the surface before returning to Earth after 8 days. *Fun Fact: Apollo 10 set the record for the highest speed ever attained by a manned vehicle on its return from the Moon; 24,791mph on May 26, 1969.*
25	The movie Midnight Cowboy, directed by John Schlesinger and starring Jon Voight and Dustin Hoffman, premieres in New York City. The film goes on to win the 1970 Academy Award for Best Picture.
30	Mario Andretti wins the 53rd Indianapolis 500. *Fun Fact: Andretti is one of only two drivers to have won races in Formula One, IndyCar, World Sportscar Championship and NASCAR (the other is Dan Gurney).*

JUN

3	While operating in the South China Sea on SEATO manoeuvres, the Australian aircraft carrier HMAS Melbourne accidentally rams and slices into the American destroyer USS Frank E. Evans. 74 American seamen are killed.
7	The Johnny Cash Show is broadcast for the first time on ABC; the 58-episode series would run until March 31, 1971.
8	President Nixon and South Vietnamese President Nguyễn Văn Thiệu meet at Midway Island. Nixon announces that 25,000 troops will be withdrawn from Vietnam by September.
20-22	An estimated 200,000 music fans attend The Newport Pop Festival (Newport '69) in Northridge, California. *Fun Fact: The 1968 event held in Costa Mesa, California, was the first ever music concert to have more than 100,000 paid attendees.*
23	Warren E. Burger is sworn in as Chief Justice of the United States by retiring Chief Justice Earl Warren. Burger remains in office until September 26, 1986.
28	A series of spontaneous violent demonstrations by members of the gay (LGBT) community at the Stonewall Inn in the Greenwich Village neighborhood of Manhattan, New York City, mark the start of the modern gay rights movement in the U.S.

JUL

4	The Zodiac Killer shoots 19 year old Michael Mageau and 22 year old Darlene Ferrin in Vallejo, California. Ferrin is pronounced dead on her arrival at hospital.
4-5	150,000 fans attend the Atlanta Pop Festival. Over 20 musical acts, including Led Zeppelin and Janis Joplin, perform in temperatures nearing 100°F.
7	The very first U.S. troop withdrawal from Vietnam occurs as 814 men from the 9th Infantry Division leave Saigon to go home.
14	Easy Rider, directed by Dennis Hopper and starring himself, Peter Fonda and Jack Nicholson, is released. *Fun Facts: The film grossed $60 million worldwide (from a filming budget of no more than $400,000) and was added to the Library of Congress National Film Registry in 1998.*
14	The $500, $1,000, $5,000 and $10,000 bills are officially discontinued by the Federal Reserve but still technically remain legal tender.

July 16 - Apollo 11 astronauts Neil Armstrong (Commander), Michael Collins (Command Module Pilot) and Buzz Aldrin (Lunar Module Pilot) are launched by a 363ft tall Saturn V rocket toward the Moon from Kennedy Space Center on Merritt Island, Florida. After travelling for three days they enter into lunar orbit and on July 20, Armstrong and Aldrin transfer into the lunar module Eagle. Eagle then descends to the Moon's surface and lands in the Sea of Tranquility. On July 21, six hours after landing, an estimated 500 million people worldwide watch in awe as Neil Armstrong steps off Eagle's footpad onto the Moon and utters the now famous words, "That's one small step for [a] man, one giant leap for mankind". Twenty minutes after taking his historic first steps on the Moon he is joined by Buzz Aldrin and they proceed to collect 47.5lb of lunar material to bring back to Earth. Armstrong and Aldrin spend a total of 21.5 hours on the Moon's surface before re-joining Michael Collins in the orbiting command module Columbia. The astronauts then jettison Eagle before blasting out on a trajectory back to Earth. They splash down in the Pacific Ocean on July 24, and are immediately placed in biological isolation for several days (on the off chance they may have brought back germs from the Moon).

17	The New York Times publicly takes back the ridicule of rocket scientist Robert H. Goddard after they published (on January 13, 1920) that spaceflight was impossible.
18	Senator Edward M. Kennedy drives off a bridge into the tide-swept Poucha Pond on his way home from a party on Chappaquiddick Island, Massachusetts. Mary Jo Kopechne, a former campaign aide to his brother, dies in the submerged car.

JUL

25	President Nixon declares the Nixon Doctrine, stating that the U.S. now expects its Asian allies to be in charge of their own security in general, but states that the U.S. would act as a nuclear umbrella when requested.
28	The Baseball Hall of Fame's membership grows to 114 as Roy Campanella, Stan Musial, Waite Hoyt and Stan Coveleski are enshrined in front of several thousand fans on a gray, wet day in Cooperstown, New York.
31	Elvis Presley performs his first live concert in 8 years in front of 2,000 people at the International Hotel, Las Vegas.

AUG

5	NASA's Mariner 7, whose mission goal is to study the surface and atmosphere of Mars, makes its closest fly-by of the planet - 2,130mi (3,430km).
9	Members of Manson Family invade the home of actress Sharon Tate and her husband Roman Polanski in Los Angeles. The followers kill Tate and her friends; Folgers coffee heiress Abigail Folger, Wojciech Frykowski, Hollywood hairstylist Jay Sebring and Steven Parent, who was visiting the Polanski's caretaker.
12	The Haunted Mansion attraction opens at Disneyland in Anaheim, California. Later versions of the ride would also open in Florida, Tokyo and Paris.
10	The Manson Family strike again killing supermarket executive Leno LaBianca and his wife Rosemary.
13	In recognition of their achievements the Apollo 11 crew ride in parades through New York, Chicago, and Los Angeles. Whilst in Los Angeles there is also an official State Dinner at the Century Plaza Hotel to celebrate the flight. The dinner is attended by members of Congress, 44 governors, the U.S. Chief Justice and ambassadors from 83 nations. President Nixon and Vice President Spiro T. Agnew honor each astronaut by presenting them with the Presidential Medal of Freedom. This day of celebration is to be the beginning of a 45-day 'Giant Leap' tour which will take the astronauts to 25 foreign countries and include visits with many prominent world leaders.

August 15-18 - The Woodstock music festival is held on a 600-acre dairy farm in the Catskill Mountains northwest of New York City. Attracting an audience of more than 400,000 many of the most famous musicians of the time turn up and play during the rainy weekend, artists such as; Ravi Shankar, Joan Baez, Santana, Grateful Dead, Creedence Clearwater Revival, Janis Joplin with The Kozmic Blues Band, Sly & the Family Stone, The Who, Jefferson Airplane, Joe Cocker, The Band, Blood Sweat & Tears, Crosby Stills Nash & Young, and Jimi Hendrix. *Fun Fact: Woodstock is widely regarded as a pivotal moment in popular music history and as such, in 2017, the festival site was listed on the U.S. National Register of Historic Places.*

AUG

17	Category 5 hurricane Camille hits the Mississippi coast killing 259 people and causing $1.43 billion in damages.
20	Florissant Fossil Beds National Monument is established in Teller County, Colorado. *Fun Fact: The Monuments' location is famous for abundant, and exceptionally well preserved, insect and plant fossils dating back 34 million years.*

SEP

1	Jerry Lewis' 4th Muscular Dystrophy telethon raises $2,039,139; an increase of over 45% on the previous year.
2	Chemical Bank installs the first U.S. automatic teller machine (ATM) - designed by Donald Wetzel and his company Docutel - at its branch in Rockville Centre, New York. The first ATMs were designed to dispense a fixed amount of cash when a user inserted a specially coded card. A Chemical Bank advertisement at the time boasted "On Sept. 2 our bank will open at 9:00 and never close again".
5	My Lai Massacre: Lieutenant William Calley is charged with 6 counts of premeditated murder for the deaths of 109 unarmed South Vietnamese civilians in My Lai on March 16, 1968. On March 29, 1971, he is convicted murdering 22 and sentenced to life imprisonment, and hard labor, at Fort Leavenworth. Instead of prison he is put under house arrest at Fort Benning (under orders from President Nixon) and is released just three and a half years later.
6	The children's TV series H.R. Pufnstuf begins its run on NBC. Produced by Sid and Marty Krofft, all seventeen episodes are shot at Paramount Studios.
9	Allegheny Airlines Flight 853, a McDonnell Douglas DC-9 passenger jet, collides in mid-air with a Piper PA-28 light aircraft near Fairland, Indiana. All 83 occupants of both aircraft are killed in the accident.
13	The Plastic Ono Band, featuring John Lennon, Yoko Ono, Eric Clapton, Klaus Voormann and Alan White, make their first live performance at the Toronto Rock and Roll Revival music festival.

September 13 - Hanna-Barbera's 'Scooby-Doo Where Are You' debuts on CBS. The series centers on four teenagers (Fred Jones, Daphne Blake, Velma Dinkley and Shaggy Rogers) and a Great Dane named Scooby-Doo. The group travel in a van named the Mystery Machine, solving mysteries involving several local legends; in doing so, they discover that the perpetrator is almost invariably a disguised person who seeks to exploit the legend for personal gain.

SEP

20	The very last Warner Brothers cartoon of the original Merrie Melodies series, Injun Trouble featuring Cool Cat, is released. *Fun Fact: This was the 1000th cartoon short released by Warner Brothers and ended a run which had lasted since 1931.*
23	Butch Cassidy and the Sundance Kid, starring Paul Newman and Robert Redford, premieres in Los Angeles. *Fun Facts: The film won four Academy Awards and in 2003 was selected for the U.S. National Film Registry (by the Library of Congress) for being, 'culturally, historically, or aesthetically significant'.*
24	The Chicago Eight (later Chicago Seven) trial begins in Chicago, Illinois. The eight defendants are charged by the federal government with conspiracy, inciting to riot, and other charges related to anti-Vietnam War and countercultural protests that took place in Chicago on the occasion of the 1968 Democratic National Convention. After the federal trial resulting in both acquittals and convictions, followed by appeals and reversals, some of the eight defendants were finally convicted - all of the convictions were eventually reversed.
26	The Brady Bunch premieres on ABC. The series airs for five seasons and 117 episodes before it is canceled in March 1974.
27	The Zodiac Killer attacks Bryan Calvin Hartnell, 20, and Cecelia Ann Shepard, 22, at Lake Berryessa in Napa County. Hartnell survives eight stab wounds to the back, but Shepard dies as a result of her injuries on September 29, 1969.

OCT

1	A 5.6Mw earthquake strikes the city of Santa Rosa, California. This is followed two hours later by a 5.7Mw shock and at least 200 aftershocks. The earthquakes cause the death of one person and damage estimated at around $8.35 million.
2	A 1.2 megaton thermonuclear device is tested at Amchitka Island, Alaska. Code-named Project Milrow, it is the 11th detonation of Operation Mandrel's (1969-1970) underground nuclear test series.
8 - 11	Days of Rage: In Chicago the National Guard is called in to control demonstrations involving the radical Weathermen.
11	The Zodiac Killer shoots and kills taxi cab driver Paul Lee Stine, 29, in the Presidio Heights neighborhood in San Francisco.
15	Hundreds of thousands of people take part in demonstrations across the U.S. in the Moratorium to End the War in Vietnam.
15	The 3rd Country Music Association Awards are held at the Ryman Auditorium in Nashville, Tennessee. Johnny Cash and Tammy Wynette are presented with the awards for male and female vocalists of the year.
16	The New York Mets win the World Series beating the heavily favored Baltimore Orioles 4-1 to accomplish one of the greatest upsets in World Series history.
17	Fourteen black athletes are kicked off the University of Wyoming football team by their coach Lloyd Eaton; the players had dared to ask if they could wear black armbands during a game in a protest against discrimination.
17	Willard S. Boyle and George Smith come up with an idea for the first charged-couple device (CCD) at Bell Laboratories in Murray Hill, New Jersey. *Fun Fact: The CCD became used in digital cameras and their invention was recognised with Boyle and Smith being rewarded with a share of the 2009 Nobel Prize in Physics.*
29	The first message is sent over ARPANET (the forerunner of the internet) between the University of California, Los Angeles and Stanford Research Institute - it is sent by student programmer Charley Kline.
31	Wal-Mart, founded by Sam Walton in 1962, is incorporated as Walmart Inc. *Fun Fact: As of January 31, 2018, Walmart has 11,718 stores and clubs in 28 countries, operating under 59 different names.*

3	President Nixon delivers a televised evening address from his White House office. In the address he asks the 'silent majority' to join him in solidarity with the Vietnam War effort and to support his policies. Vice President Spiro T. Agnew denounces the President's critics as, "an effete corps of impudent snobs who characterize themselves as intellectuals".
10	The educational children's television series Sesame Street premieres on PBS TV. *Fun Facts: Since Sesame Street was first aired in 1969 there have been 48 seasons and 4,480 episodes of the show; it has also won 167 Emmy Awards and 8 Grammy Awards - more than any other children's show.*
12	My Lai Massacre: Independent investigative journalist Seymour Hersh breaks the My Lai story describing how hundreds of unarmed Vietnamese civilians were murdered by U.S. soldiers in March 1968. His investigation wins him the 1970 Pulitzer Prize.
15	The Soviet submarine K-19 collides with the American submarine USS Gato in the Barents Sea. Gato is relatively undamaged and continues with her patrol but K-19 has to return to port having destroyed the bow sonar systems and mangled the covers of the forward torpedo tubes.

November 15 - In a second Moratorium march in Washington, D.C., antiwar activists stream down Pennsylvania Avenue calling for a rapid withdrawal of troops from Vietnam. Three drummers lead the procession followed by people carrying 11 coffins bearing names of the dead. Behind these are many rows of marchers shouting, "Peace now! Peace now!" The official police estimate puts the crowd to be at least 250,000 strong (although alternative estimates from the time state that the number of protesters was actually more like 500,000). President Nixon said of the march, "Now, I understand that there has been, and continues to be, opposition to the war in Vietnam on the campuses and also in the nation. As far as this kind of activity is concerned, we expect it; however under no circumstances will I be affected whatever by it".

15	Dave Thomas opens his first Wendy's restaurant in a former steakhouse in downtown Columbus, Ohio. *Fun Fact: Thomas called it Wendy's after his 8-year-old daughter Melinda Lou, who was nicknamed Wendy by her siblings.*

NOV

17	Cold War: Negotiators from the Soviet Union and the United States meet in Helsinki to begin the SALT I conferences. Aimed at limiting the number of strategic weapons, an agreement between the two sides is eventually signed on May 26, 1972.
19	Apollo 12 astronauts Charles Conrad and Alan Bean land at Oceanus Procellarum (Ocean of Storms) to become the third and fourth humans to walk on the Moon. The Command Module Pilot was Richard F. Gordon Jr. who remained in lunar orbit aboard the Yankee Clipper.
19	President Nixon meets with Japanese Prime Minister Eisaku Sato in the Oval Office for discussions on negotiating a return of Okinawa Island to Japan.
21	The U.S. Senate votes down the Supreme Court nomination of Clement Haynsworth by of 55 to 45, the first such rejection since 1930. Nixon eventually nominates Harry Blackmun who is later confirmed by the Senate.

DEC

1	Vietnam War: The first draft lottery since World War II is held to determine the order of call to military service for men born from 1944 to 1950.
6	The Altamont Free Concert is held at the Altamont Speedway in northern California. 300,000 fans attend the rock concert to see the likes of Santana, Jefferson Airplane, The Flying Burrito Brothers, Crosby, Stills, Nash & Young, and the Rolling Stones. During the event scores fans are injured, numerous cars are stolen and then abandoned, and there is extensive property damage. The event also sees the stabbing to death of Meredith Hunter by Hells Angel Alan Passaro, and three accidental deaths: two caused by a hit-and-run car accident, and one by LSD-induced drowning in an irrigation canal.
12	The 1968 Olympic gold medallist Bill Toomey achieves a world record decathlon score of 8417 points in Los Angeles.

December 14 - The Jackson 5 make their first appearance on the iconic Ed Sullivan Show where a 10 year old Michael Jackson and his 4 brothers, Jackie, Tito, Jermaine and Marlon, dazzle and amaze the audience. The exposure from the show elevates the group's national profile to another level and captures the hearts of fans from around the world.

30 WORLDWIDE NEWS & EVENTS

1. January 15 - The Soviet Union launches Soyuz 5, which docks with Soyuz 4 the following day for a transfer of crew. It is the first-ever docking of two manned spacecraft and the first-ever transfer of crew from one space vehicle to another; it is also the only time a transfer has been accomplished with a spacewalk. The two spacecraft undock and return to Earth on January 18.
2. January 22 - An assassination attempt is carried out on Leonid Brezhnev by deserter Viktor Ilyin. One person is killed and several are injured; Brezhnev escapes unharmed.

3. January 30 - The Beatles - John Lennon, Paul McCartney, George Harrison and Ringo Starr - play live for one last time with an impromptu gig on the roof of their Apple headquarters in Saville Row, Mayfair, London. The outing is abruptly cut short by police who object to the noise, but not before they manage to thrill Londoners on adjacent rooftops and on the streets below. The 42-minute rooftop 'concert' is the first live gig since the band stopped touring in 1966 and ends with Lennon quipping, "I hope we passed the audition".

4. February 4 - Yasser Arafat is elected Palestine Liberation Organization leader at the Palestinian National Congress held in Cairo.
5. March 2 - The Anglo-French supersonic airliner Concorde makes its maiden flight after two previous attempts were aborted due to bad weather. Spontaneous applause and cheers broke out from observers as the French-built prototype of the supersonic transport (SST) took off from Toulouse Airport at around 3.30pm; it circled for just 27 minutes before landing due to further weather concerns. Test pilot Andre Turcat said that the flight was "as perfect as we had expected", but warned that Concorde was far from being the finished article.
6. March 4 - The Kray twins, Ronnie and Reggie, are both found guilty of murdering Jack 'the Hat' McVitie at the Old Bailey in London, England; Ronnie was also found guilty of murdering George Cornell. A day later they are sentenced to life imprisonment by Mr Justice Melford Stevenson with a recommended minimum of thirty years - the sentences are the longest ever passed at the Old Bailey for murder. The Kray's elder brother Charles was also found guilty and jailed for 10 years for being an accessory in the murder of McVitie.
7. March 16 - Viasa Flight 742 hits a series of power lines shortly after taking off for Miami and crashes into a neighbourhood in Maracaibo, Venezuela; all 84 people on board the DC-9 jet are killed, along with 71 people on the ground.
8. March 17 - Golda Meir becomes the first female prime minister of Israel.
9. March 29 - Lulu, representing the United Kingdom with the song 'Boom Bang-a-Bang', shares first place in the Eurovision Song Contest in a four-way tie with France, the Netherlands and the host country, Spain.

CONTINUED

10. April 22 - The United Kingdom's Robin Knox-Johnston becomes the first person to perform a single-handed non-stop circumnavigation of the globe. Of the 9 competitors in Sunday Times Golden Globe Race he was the only finisher and was awarded both the trophy, and £5,000 prize money.

11. April 28 - Charles de Gaulle steps down as president of France after suffering defeat in a referendum the day before. The proposed referendum reforms, rejected by 52.4% of voters, would have led to government decentralization and changes to the Senate.

12. May 2 - Cunard's ocean liner Queen Elizabeth 2 departs Southampton, England on her maiden voyage to New York. The ship was built by John Brown and Company at their shipyard in Clydebank, Scotland, for an agreed price of £25,427,000. She was launched and named on September 20, 1967 by Queen Elizabeth II using the same pair of gold scissors her mother and grandmother had used to launch Cunard's Queen Elizabeth and Queen Mary respectively. On May 3, 1982 she was requisitioned by the British government for service as a troop carrier in the Falklands War, and since April 18, 2018 has been operating as a floating hotel in Dubai. *Photo: The QE2 arriving in New York on May 7, 1969.*

CONTINUED

13. May 16 - Venera 5, a Soviet atmospheric space probe weighing 893lb (405kg), is jettisoned from its main spacecraft on its way towards the surface of Venus. A parachute opens to slow the rate of descent and for 53 minutes data from the Venusian atmosphere is returned. The probe finally succumbs to high temperatures and pressure as it nears the surface of Venus.
14. May 23 - The Who release their fourth studio album, the concept album Tommy. *Fun Fact: Tommy has to date sold over 20 million copies globally.*
15. June 20 - Georges Pompidou is elected President of France - he would remain as President of the French Republic until his death on April 2, 1974.
16. June 30 - The Government of Spain formally returns the province of Ifni, which they had occupied since 1860, to Morocco.

17. July 3 - Brian Jones (b. Lewis Brian Hopkin Jones; February 28, 1942) who founded and was the original leader of the Rolling Stones dies. Initially a slide guitarist, Jones played a wide variety of instruments on Rolling Stones recordings and in concerts; instruments such as rhythm and lead guitar, piano, organ, marimba, harmonica, sitar, recorder, saxophone and oboe amongst others. Andrew Loog Oldham's arrival as manager of the Stones marked the beginning of Jones' slow estrangement. Oldham pushed the band into a musical direction at odds with Jones's blues background. Around the same time Jones developed a drug problem and his performance in the studio became increasingly unreliable, leading to a diminished role within the band he founded. The Rolling Stones asked Jones to leave in June 1969 and guitarist Mick Taylor took his place in the group. Jones died less than a month later after drowning in his swimming pool whilst under the influence of drugs.

18. July 14 - The Soccer War (also known as the 100 Hour War) begins when the Salvadoran military launches an attack against Honduras after existing tensions between the two countries coincided with rioting during a 1970 FIFA World Cup qualifier. The Organization of American States (OAS) negotiates a cease-fire on the night of July 18 which takes full effect from July 20.
19. July 19 - British rower and adventurer John Fairfax lands in Hollywood Beach, Florida, and becomes the first person to row across an ocean solo; he had left Gran Canaria on January 20 and had spent a total of 180 days at sea on board his 25ft ocean rowboat Britannia.
20. August 8 - At 11:35am photographer Iain Macmillan takes a photo of The Beatles for their new album on a zebra crossing outside EMI Studios in Abbey Road. *Fun Fact: In December 2010 the crossing was given British grade II listed status for its 'cultural and historical importance'.*
21. August 12 - Rioting breaks out in Derry, Northern Ireland, in the Battle of the Bogside - the first major confrontation of The Troubles.

CONTINUED

22. August 13 - The Taoiseach of the Republic of Ireland, Jack Lynch, makes a speech on RTÉ television stating that his government "can no longer stand by and see innocent people injured and perhaps worse". He also says that the Stormont government is no longer in control of the situation and that London should request the United Nations send a peacekeeping force to Northern Ireland.
23. August 14 - The British Government sends troops into Northern Ireland in what it says is a 'limited operation' to restore law and order. It follows three days and two nights of violence in the mainly-Catholic Bogside area of Londonderry.
24. Colonel Muammar Gaddafi deposes King Idris in the Libyan revolution.
25. October 5 - Monty Python's Flying Circus' first episode is broadcast on the BBC. It stars Terry Jones, Michael Palin, Eric Idle, John Cleese, Graham Chapman and American-born Terry Gilliam.
26. Scottish Formula One driver Jackie Stewart wins the first of his three World Drivers Championships. Driving for Matra International he took six of the eleven Grand Prix's and with 63 points was an impressive 26 points in front of second placed Jacky Ickx from Belgium.
27. October 21 - Willy Brandt, leader of the Social Democratic Party, becomes Chancellor of West Germany.
28. November 19 - The Benny Hill Show, first broadcast on the BBC in 1955, premieres on the British ITV network station Thames Television. The show would run until 1989 before it is cancelled due to declining (UK) ratings and large production costs of £450,000 per episode. *Fun Fact: At the time the Benny Hill Show was cancelled in 1989 it was being aired in 97 countries around the world.*

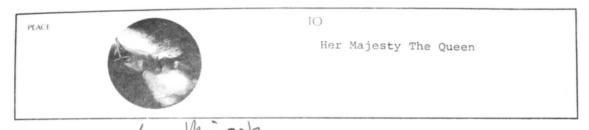

Your Majesty

I am returning this MBE in protest against Britain's involvement in the Nigeria-Biafra thing, against our support of America in Vietnam and against Cold Turkey slipping down the charts.

with love
John Lennon of Bag

29. November 25 - John Lennon returns his 'Most Excellent Order of the British Empire' (MBE) decoration in protest against the British government's involvement in Biafra, their support of the war in Vietnam, and the disappointing performance of his second solo single Cold Turkey. *Photo: A draft (valued at £60,000) of the letter sent by Lennon when he returned his MBE; the actual letter remains in the British Royal archives.*

30. December 18 - The sixth James Bond film, On Her Majesty's Secret Service, premieres at the Odeon Leicester Square in London. It stars Australian actor George Lazenby as Bond alongside 31-year old Avengers actress Diana Rigg.

BIRTHS
U.S. PERSONALITIES BORN IN 1969

Verne Jay Troyer
January 1, 1969 -
April 21, 2018

Actor, comedian and stunt performer best known for playing Mini-Me in the Austin Powers film series. He was notable for having been only 2ft 8in (81cm) tall making him one of the shortest men in the world. Troyer's other work included portraying the goblin Griphook in Harry Potter And The Sorcerer's Stone (2001), and playing the role of Percy in The Imaginarium Of Doctor Parnassus (2009). He also made several appearances as himself in a number of reality television series.

Marla Lee Runyan
(Lonergan)
January 4, 1969

Legally blind track and field athlete, road runner and marathon runner. Runyan won four gold medals at the 1992 Summer Paralympics, in the long jump and the 100m, 200m, and 400m races, and at the 1996 Paralympics took silver in the shot put and gold in the pentathlon. Her career in able-bodied events began in 1999 and she was placed 8th in the 1,500m final at the 2000 Sydney Olympics - this made her the first legally blind athlete to compete in the Olympics.

Brian Hugh Warner
January 5, 1969

Singer, songwriter, musician, composer, actor, painter, author and former music journalist known by his stage name Marilyn Manson. As the lead singer of the band Marilyn Manson, which he co-founded with guitarist Daisy Berkowitz, he has been nominated for four Grammy Awards, had two No.1 albums, seen three albums awarded platinum status and three more gold. Manson was ranked No.44 in the 'Top 100 Heavy Metal Vocalists' by the music magazine Hit Parader.

David Eric Grohl
January 14, 1969

Musician, singer, songwriter, record producer, and film director. He was the longest-serving drummer for the grunge band Nirvana and is the founder and frontman of the rock band Foo Fighters. He is also the drummer and co-founder of the rock supergroup Them Crooked Vultures, and wrote the music and performed all the instruments for his short-lived side projects Late! and Probot. In 2014, as a member of Nirvana, Grohl was inducted into the Rock and Roll Hall of Fame.

Roy Levesta Jones Jr.
January 16, 1969

Former professional boxer, boxing commentator, boxing trainer, rapper and actor who holds dual American and Russian citizenship. Jones competed in boxing from 1989 to 2018, and is a multiple time world champion in four weight classes having held titles at middleweight, super middleweight, light heavyweight, and heavyweight; he is also the only boxer in history to start his professional career at light middleweight and go on to win a heavyweight title.

David Michael Bautista Jr.
January 18, 1969

Actor, retired professional wrestler, mixed martial artist and bodybuilder. From 2000 to 2010 and 2013 to 2014, he was signed to WWE under the ring name Batista, where he became a six-time world champion, winning WWE's World Heavyweight Championship four times and the WWE Championship twice. Bautista holds the record for the longest reign as World Heavyweight Champion at 282 days and also headlined WrestleMania 21, one of the top five highest-grossing pay-per-view events in professional wrestling history.

Robert Barisford 'Bobby' Brown
February 5, 1969

Singer, songwriter, dancer and actor. Brown started his career in the R&B and pop group New Edition, from its inception in 1978 until his exit from the group in 1985. He then started a solo career and enjoyed success with his second album in 1988, Don't Be Cruel, which spawned a number of hit singles including My Prerogative, and the Grammy Award-winning Every Little Step. In 2005 Brown starred in the highly rated reality show Being Bobby Brown with his then wife Whitney Houston.

Jennifer Joanna Aniston
February 11, 1969

Actress, film producer and businesswoman who gained worldwide recognition for portraying Rachel Green on the television sitcom Friends (1994-2004). The role earned her a number of accolades including a Primetime Emmy Award, a Golden Globe Award and a Screen Actors Guild Award. In 2012 she received a star on the Hollywood Walk of Fame and is today one of the highest-paid actresses in Hollywood; Aniston has a net worth estimated at around $200 million (2017).

Paul Stephen Rudd
April 6, 1969

Actor, comedian, writer and producer who made his acting debut in 1992 in NBC's drama series Sisters. He is known for his starring roles in films such as Clueless (1995), Romeo + Juliet (1996), Anchorman: The Legend of Ron Burgundy (2004), The 40-Year-Old Virgin (2005) and The Fundamentals Of Caring (2016). He is also known for portraying the superhero Ant-Man in the Marvel Cinematic Universe. Rudd received a star on the Hollywood Walk of Fame on July 1, 2015.

Renée Kathleen Zellweger
April 25, 1969

Actress and producer who has received numerous accolades including an Academy Award, a BAFTA Award, three Golden Globe Awards and three Screen Actors Guild Awards. Her first major film role came in Texas Chainsaw Massacre: The Next Generation (1994), which she followed with a critically acclaimed appearance in Empire Records (1995). Notable movies include Jerry Maguire (1996), Nurse Betty (2000), Chicago (2002), Cold Mountain (2003), Cinderella Man (2005) and the Bridget Jones trilogy of films.

Emmitt James Smith III
May 15, 1969

Former college and professional football running back who became the NFL's all-time leading rusher during his fifteen seasons in the league (1990-2004). Smith played for three Super Bowl-winning Dallas Cowboys teams and holds the record for career rushing touchdowns with 164. He is also one of only two non-kickers in NFL history to score more than 1,000 career points (the other being Jerry Rice). Smith was inducted into the College Football Hall of Fame in 2006 and the Pro Football Hall of Fame in 2010.

Cathy Anne McMorris Rodgers
May 22, 1969

Politician who has served as the U.S. Representative for Washington's 5th congressional district since 2005 and is the highest ranking Republican woman in Congress (serving as Chair of the House Republican Conference). Her career started when she was hired by State Representative Bob Morton in 1991, serving as his campaign manager and later his legislative assistant. She became a member of the state legislature when she was appointed to the Washington House of Representatives in 1994.

Dolores Janney 'Jenni' Rivera Saavedra
July 2, 1969 -
December 9, 2012

Singer, songwriter, actress, television producer, spokesperson, philanthropist and entrepreneur known for her work within the Banda and Ranchera music genres. In life and in death she has been labeled as the most important female figure, and top selling female artist, in the Mexican music genre. Rivera has a star on the Las Vegas Walk of Stars, has sold more than 20 million records worldwide, and has garnered nominations and awards from Latin music's most prestigious accolades.

Jennifer Lynn Lopez
July 24, 1969

Singer, actress, dancer and producer who began appearing as a Fly Girl dancer on Fox's In Living Color in 1991. In 1993 she decided to pursue an acting career and gained her first leading role in Selena (1997). For this she received a Golden Globe nomination and became the first Latin actress to earn over $1 million for a film. She ventured into the music industry with her debut studio album On The 6 (1999) and today has estimated global sales of 80 million records. Lopez is regarded as the most influential Latin performer in the U.S.

Paul Michael Levesque
July 27, 1969

Business executive, professional wrestler and actor better known by the ring name Triple H (an abbreviation of his original WWE ring name Hunter Hearst Helmsley). He has been the Executive Vice President of Talent, Live Events and Creative for WWE since 2013, as well as being the founder and senior producer of NXT. Over the course of his career Levesque has held a total of 25 championships including nine reigns as WWF/WWE Champion and five as WWE's World Heavyweight Champion.

Donald Edmond Wahlberg Jr.
August 17, 1969

Songwriter, actor, and record and film producer who is a founding member of the boy band New Kids on the Block. Outside music he has had roles in the Saw films and others such as The Sixth Sense (1999), Dreamcatcher (2003), and Righteous Kill (2008). On television Wahlberg has appeared in the World War II miniseries Band Of Brothers (2001), the crime drama Boomtown (2002-2003) and the drama series Blue Bloods (2010-). He also produces and stars in Wahlburgers on A&E TV.

Christian Michael Leonard Slater
August 18, 1969

Actor and producer who made his film debut with a leading role in The Legend Of Billie Jean (1985). He gained wider recognition as Jason Dean in Heathers (1988) and in the 1990s starred in many big budget films including Robin Hood: Prince of Thieves (1991), Interview with the Vampire (1994), FernGully: The Last Rainforest (1992), Broken Arrow (1996) and Hard Rain (1998). Since 2000 he has combined work in the film business with television and currently has the titular role in the USA Network series Mr. Robot (2015-).

Matthew Langford Perry
August 19, 1969

American-Canadian actor, comedian and playwright known for his role as Chandler Bing on the NBC television sitcom Friends (1994-2004). Along with starring in a number of other television series such as Studio 60 On The Sunset Strip (2006-2007), Perry has appeared in movies including Fools Rush In (1997), The Whole Nine Yards (2000) and 17 Again (2009). In 2010 he expanded his résumé to include both video games and voiceover work when he voiced Benny in the video game Fallout: New Vegas.

Sheryl Kara Sandberg
August 28, 1969

Technology executive, activist and author who is the chief operating officer of Facebook and founder of Leanin.org. Before she joined Facebook Sandberg was vice president of global online sales and operations at Google, and was involved in launching Google's philanthropic arm Google.org. Before that Sandberg served as Chief of Staff for U.S. Secretary of the Treasury Lawrence Summers. In 2012 she was named in the Time 100, an annual list of the most influential people in the world according to Time magazine.

Thomas Jacob 'Jack' Black
August 28, 1969

Actor, comedian, musician, singer and songwriter. His acting career has been extensive but he is probably best known for his roles in Shallow Hal (2001), School Of Rock (2003), King Kong (2005), the Kung Fu Panda franchise (2008-2016), Tropic Thunder (2008), Gulliver's Travels (2010), Goosebumps (2015), and Jumanji: Welcome To The Jungle (2017). In music Black is the lead vocalist of the comedic rock duo Tenacious D which he formed in 1994 with friend Kyle Gass.

Gwen Renée Stefani
October 3, 1969

Singer, songwriter and fashion designer who is a co-founder and the lead vocalist of the band No Doubt. Stefani has won three Grammy Awards and has received various accolades including an American Music Award, a Brit Award, a World Music Award and two Billboard Music Awards. Including her work with No Doubt, she has sold more than 30 million albums worldwide. In 2003 she launched her clothing line L.A.M.B. and expanded her collection with the 2005 Harajuku Lovers line, inspired by Japanese culture and fashion.

Brett Lorenzo Favre
October 10, 1969

Former football quarterback who spent the majority of his 20-year career with the Green Bay Packers of the NFL. He was the first NFL quarterback to pass for 500 touchdowns, throw for 70,000 yards, complete 6,000 passes and attempt 10,000 passes. Favre's eleven Pro Bowl invitations is the third most among quarterbacks in NFL history and he is the only player to win the Associated Press NFL Most Valuable Player Award three consecutive times (1995-1997). Favre was inducted into the Pro Football Hall of Fame in 2016.

Martha 'Martie' Elenor Erwin
October 12, 1969

Musician who is a founding member of both the female alternative country band Dixie Chicks and country blue grass duo Court Yard Hounds. Erwin won awards in the National Fiddle Championships while still a teenager and is accomplished on several other instruments including the mandolin, viola, double bass and guitar. The Dixie Chicks have won 13 Grammy Awards (including five in 2007 for their seventh studio album, Taking The Long Way) and have sold over 30 million albums worldwide.

Sean John Combs
November 4, 1969

Rapper, singer, songwriter, actor, record producer and entrepreneur also known by his stage names Puff Daddy, Puffy, Diddy, P. Diddy, Love and Brother Love. Combs worked as a talent director at Uptown Records before founding his label Bad Boy Entertainment in 1993. In 1997 he released his debut album No Way Out which has been certified seven times platinum. The winner of three Grammy Awards and two MTV Video Music Awards, Forbes has estimated his net worth at $825 million (2018).

Ellen Kathleen Pompeo
November 10, 1969

Actress, director and producer who is one of the highest paid television stars after signing a $20 million annual contract with the American Broadcasting Company in late 2017. She made her screen debut in NBC's legal drama Law & Order and gained wide recognition for her starring role in Brad Silberling's drama film Moonlight Mile (2002). Pompeo was then cast in ABC's popular medical drama Grey's Anatomy and she has since garnered worldwide recognition for her portrayal of the title character Dr. Meredith Grey.

George Kenneth Griffey Jr.
November 21, 1969

Former professional baseball outfielder who played 22 years in MLB. He spent most of his career with the Seattle Mariners and Cincinnati Reds, and was a 13-time All-Star. He is one of the most prolific home run hitters in baseball history; his 630 home runs rank as the seventh-most in MLB history and he is tied for the record of most consecutive games with a home run (eight, with Don Mattingly and Dale Long). Griffey was also an exceptional defender and won 10 Gold Glove Awards in center field.

Shawn Corey Carter
December 4, 1969

Rapper, songwriter, record producer and entrepreneur known professionally as Jay-Z. One of the world's best-selling music artists and one of the most acclaimed rappers of all-time, he has received 21 Grammy Awards (tied with Kanye West for the most by a rapper). He also holds the record for the most No.1 albums by a solo artist on the Billboard 200 with 13. Carter, who married singer Beyoncé in 2008, has an estimated individual net worth of $900 million making him the richest hip hop artist in the world.

Notable American Deaths

Jan 24	Jonathan Thompson Walton 'Tom' Zachary (b. May 7, 1896) - Professional baseball pitcher who had a 19-year career in MLB that lasted from 1918 to 1936.
Jan 29	Allen Welsh Dulles (b. April 7, 1893) - Diplomat and lawyer who became the first civilian Director of Central Intelligence, and its longest-serving director to date.
Feb 5	Thelma Ritter (b. February 14, 1902) - Actress, best known for her comedic roles as working-class characters and her strong New York accent. She received six Academy Award nominations for Best Supporting Actress throughout her career - more than any other actress in history.
Feb 14	Vito 'Don Vitone' Genovese (b. November 27, 1897) - Italian-American mobster who rose to power during Prohibition as an enforcer in the Mafia. A long-time associate and childhood friend of Charles Luciano, Genovese took part in the Castellammarese War and helped shape the rise of the Mafia and organized crime in the United States. He would later lead Luciano's crime family (renamed the Genovese crime family by the authorities).
Feb 27	John Boles (b. October 28, 1895) - Singer and actor best known for playing Victor Moritz in the 1931 film Frankenstein.

March 28 - Dwight David 'Ike' Eisenhower (b. October 14, 1890) - Army general and statesman who served as the 34th President of the United States from 1953 to 1961. During World War II he was a five-star general in the U.S. Army and served as Supreme Commander of the Allied Expeditionary Forces in Europe. He was responsible for planning and supervising the invasions of North Africa in 1942-1943 and of France and Germany in 1944-1945.

Apr 10	Harley J. Earl (b. November 22, 1893) - Automotive designer and business executive who was the first designated head of design at General Motors (later becoming vice president). Amongst other things, Earl was responsible for the introduction of the 'concept car' to the automotive industry.
May 19	Coleman Randolph Hawkins (b. November 21, 1904) - Prominent jazz tenor saxophonist nicknamed 'Hawk'.
May 23	James Francis McHugh (b. July 10, 1894) - One of the U.S.'s most prolific songwriters from the 1920s to the 1950s (he is credited with writing over 500 songs). Many of his compositions were recorded by the top artists of the day including Bing Crosby, Ella Fitzgerald, Judy Garland, Adelaide Hall, Billie Holiday, Bill Kenny, Peggy Lee, Nina Simone, and Dinah Washington.
May 26	Allan Haines Lockheed (b. January 20, 1889) - Aviation pioneer who formed the Alco Hydro-Aeroplane Company (Lockheed Corporation) with his brother Malcolm.

CONTINUED

May 27	Jeffrey Hunter (b. Henry Herman McKinnies Jr.; November 25, 1926) - Film and television actor known for his roles in films such as The Searchers (1956) and King Of Kings (1961). Hunter was also known for his 1965 role as Capt. Christopher Pike in the original pilot episode of Star Trek.
Jun 8	Robert Taylor (b. Spangler Arlington Brugh; August 5, 1911) - Film and television actor who was one of the most popular leading men of his time.
Jun 14	Wynonie Harris (b. August 24, 1915) - Blues shouter and rhythm-and-blues singer of upbeat songs featuring humorous, often ribald, lyrics. He had fifteen Top 10 hits between 1946 and 1952, and is attributed by many music scholars to be one of the founding fathers of rock and roll.
Jun 21	Maureen Catherine Connolly-Brinker (b. September 17, 1934) - Tennis player known as 'Little Mo' who was the winner of nine Grand Slam singles titles in the early 1950s; in 1953 she became the first woman to win all four Grand Slam tournaments during the same calendar year. Her competitive tennis career ended in July 1954 aged just 19 after her right leg was injured in a horse riding accident.

June 22 - Judy Garland (b. Frances Ethel Gumm; June 10, 1922) - Singer, actress, dancer and vaudevillian. Garland won numerous awards throughout her career and attained international stardom as an actress in musical and dramatic roles, as a recording artist, and on the concert stage. Her most memorable movie role was that of the young Dorothy Gale in The Wizard Of Oz (1939).

Jun 24	Willy Otto Oskar Ley (b. October 2, 1906) - German-American science writer and spaceflight advocate who helped to popularize rocketry, spaceflight, and natural history. The Ley Crater on the far side of the Moon is named in his honor.
Jul 5	Thomas Leo McCarey (b. October 3, 1898) - A three time Academy Award winning film director, screenwriter and producer.
Jul 18	Mary Jo Kopechne (b. July 26, 1940) - Teacher, secretary, and political campaign specialist who died in a car that was being driven by Senator Ted Kennedy.
Jul 20	Roy Hamilton (b. April 16, 1929) - Singer who achieved his greatest commercial successes from 1954 through 1961 when he was Epic Records' most prolific artist. His two most influential recordings, You'll Never Walk Alone and Unchained Melody, became Epic's first two No.1 hits.
Aug 9	George Preston Marshall (b. October 11, 1896) - Businessman, renowned racist, and owner and president of the Washington Redskins of the NFL, from their inception in 1932 in Boston, until his death in 1969.
Aug 9	Robert Owen Lehman, Sr. (b. September 29, 1891) - Banker who was head of Lehman Brothers for decades, was a notable race-horse owner, art collector, and philanthropist.

CONTINUED

Aug 9	Sharon Marie Tate Polanski (b. January 24, 1943) - Actress and model who was hailed as one of Hollywood's most promising newcomers before being murdered by members of the Manson Family - at the time of her death she was eight-and-a-half months pregnant.

August 31 - Rocco Francis Marchegiano (b. September 1, 1923) - Professional boxer who was better known as Rocky Marciano. Marciano held the world heavyweight title from 1952 to 1956, and is the only heavyweight champion in professional boxing history to retire undefeated.

Sep 5	Joshua Daniel White (b. February 11, 1914) - Singer, guitarist, songwriter, actor and civil rights activist. He was the first black singer to give a White House command performance, the first to get a million-selling record, and the first to star in Hollywood films and on Broadway.
Oct 6	Walter Charles Hagen (b. December 21, 1892) - Professional golfer who won 11 majors and was a six-time Ryder Cup captain.
Oct 14	Arnold Charles Herber (b. April 2, 1910) - Quarterback who played in the NFL for the Green Bay Packers and New York Giants. He was inducted to the Pro Football Hall of Fame in 1966.
Oct 22	Thomas J. 'Tommy' Edwards (b. February 17, 1922) - Singer and songwriter whose best-selling record was the multi-million-selling song 'It's All in the Game'.
Nov 18	Joseph Patrick Kennedy Sr. (b. September 6, 1888) - Businessman, investor, and politician known for his high-profile positions in U.S. politics. Three of his nine children also attained distinguished political positions; President John F. Kennedy (1917-1963), Attorney General and Senator Robert F. Kennedy (1925-1968), and long-time Senator Edward M. 'Ted' Kennedy (1932-2009).
Dec 1	Samuel Gene Maghett (b. February 14, 1937) - Chicago blues musician known as Magic Sam. He was signed by Cobra Records at the age of 19 and became well known as a bluesman after the release of his first record 'All Your Love' in 1957.
Dec 4	Fred Hampton (b. August 30, 1948) - African-American activist and revolutionary, chairman of the Illinois chapter of the Black Panther Party (BPP), and deputy chairman of the national BPP.
Dec 7	Francis Joseph 'Lefty' O'Doul (b. March 4, 1897) - A Major League Baseball player who went on to become an extraordinarily successful manager in the minor leagues. He was also a vital figure in the establishment of professional baseball in Japan.
Dec 13	Raymond Ames Spruance (b. July 3, 1886) - United States Navy admiral in World War II. Spruance commanded U.S. naval forces during two of the most significant naval battles that took place in the Pacific Theatre: the Battle of Midway and the Battle of the Philippine Sea. At Midway, Spruance scored the first major victory for the U.S. over Japan, often considered the turning point of the Pacific War.

1969 TOP 10 SINGLES

Archies	No.1	Sugar Sugar
5th Dimension	No.2	Aquarius / Let The Sunshine In
Temptations	No.3	I Can't Get Next To You
Rolling Stones	No.4	Honky Tonk Women
Sly & The Family Stone	No.5	Everyday People
Tommy Roe	No.6	Dizzy
Sly & The Family Stone	No.7	Hot Fun In The Summertime
Tom Jones	No.8	I'll Never Fall In Love Again
The Foundations	No.9	Build Me Up Buttercup
Tommy James & The Shondells	No.10	Crimson And Clover

Archies
Sugar Sugar

Label:	Written by:	Length:
RCA Victor / Calendar	Andy Kim / Jeff Barry	2 mins 48 secs

The Archies were a fictional garage band founded by Archie Andrews, Reggie Mantle, Jughead Jones, Veronica Lodge and Betty Cooper, a group of adolescent characters from the animated CBS TV series The Archie Show. The fictional band's music was recorded by session musicians and featured vocalists Ron Dante and Toni Wine. Sugar, Sugar was The Archies most successful song and became one of the biggest hits of the bubble-gum pop genre that flourished from 1968 to 1973.

5th Dimension
Aquarius / Let The Sunshine In

Label:	Written by:	Length:
Soul City	MacDermot / Gerome / Rado	4 mins 49 secs

The 5th Dimension are a popular music vocal group whose song 'Aquarius / Let the Sunshine In' peaked at No.1 for six weeks on the Billboard Hot 100 Singles Chart in the spring of 1969. This platinum selling hit record is a medley of two songs written for the 1967 musical Hair and is listed at No.66 on Billboard's Greatest Songs of All Time.

 ## Temptations
I Can't Get Next To You

Label:	Written by:	Length:
Gordy (Motown)	Strong / Whitfield	2 mins 53 secs

The Temptations are a vocal group who released a series of successful singles and albums with Motown Records during the 1960s and 1970s. They are among the most successful groups in popular music and their recording of 'I Can't Get Next To You' was the second of four No.1 hits to top Billboard Hot 100 record chart. Six of the many members of The Temptations (Edwards, Franklin, Kendricks, Ruffin, Otis Williams and Paul Williams) were inducted into the Rock and Roll Hall of Fame in 1989.

 ## Rolling Stones
Honky Tonk Women

Label:	Written by:	Length:
London Records	Jagger / Richards	3 mins 0 secs

The Rolling Stones were formed in London in 1962 and the line-up at the time Honky Tonk Women was released was Mick Jagger (lead vocals), Keith Richards (guitar, backing vocals), Mick Taylor (lead guitar), Bill Wyman (bass) and Charlie Watts (drums). They have to date released 30 studio albums, 23 live albums and numerous compilations with estimated total record sales in excess of 250 million units.

Sly & The Family Stone
Everyday People

Label:	Written by:	Length:
Epic	Sylvester Stewart	2 mins 18 secs

Sly and the Family Stone was a band from San Francisco that was pivotal in the development of funk, soul, rock, and psychedelic music. Active from 1966 to 1983, the core line-up was led by singer-songwriter, producer, and multi-instrumentalist Sly Stone (b. Sylvester Stewart). Everyday People was the first of three singles by the band to go to No.1 on Billboard Hot 100 chart.

Tommy Roe
Dizzy

Label:	Written by:	Length:
ABC Records	Weller / Roe	2 mins 55 secs

Thomas David 'Tommy' Roe (b. May 9, 1942) is a singer-songwriter who was widely perceived as one of the archetypal bubble-gum artists of the late 1960s. The song Dizzy, whose instrumental backing was provided by the Los Angeles session musicians the Wrecking Crew, became an international hit single reaching the No.1 spot in the U.K., Canada and the U.S.

Sly & The Family Stone
Hot Fun In The Summertime

Label:	Written by:	Length:
Epic	Sylvester Stewart	2 mins 37 secs

Hot Fun In The Summertime was released in the wake of Sly and The Family Stone's high-profile performance at Woodstock. The band was inducted into the Rock and Roll Hall of Fame in 1993 and 2010 they were ranked 43rd in Rolling Stone's 100 Greatest Artists of All Time. Sly and The Family Stone were the first major American rock group to have a racially integrated male and female line up.

Tom Jones
I'll Never Fall In Love Again

Label:	Written by:	Length:
Decca	Currie / Donegan	2 mins 55 secs

Sir Thomas Jones Woodward, OBE (b. June 7, 1940) is a Welsh singer whose career has spanned more than six decades. Known by his stage name Tom Jones, he is one of the most popular vocalists to emerge from the mid-1960s and has sold over 100 million records worldwide. I'll Never Fall In Love Again was originally recorded by Jones in 1967 and was reissued in 1969 when it reached No.6 on the Hot 100, and No.1 on the Adult Contemporary chart.

9 The Foundations
Build Me Up Buttercup

Label:	Written by:	Length:
UNI Records	D'Abo / Macaulay	2 mins 56 secs

The Foundations were a British soul band, active from 1967 to 1970, who were one of the few British acts to successfully imitate what became known as the Motown Sound. The group were the first multi-racial group to have a No.1 hit in the U.K. in the 1960's and are best known for their two biggest hits, Baby Now That I've Found You, and Build Me Up Buttercup. Build Me Up Buttercup was certified Gold by the RIAA for record sales of over a million U.S. copies.

---

10 Tommy James & The Shondells
Crimson And Clover

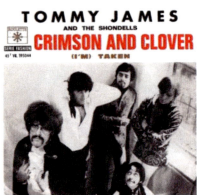 

Label:	Written by:	Length:
Roulette	Lucia / James	5 mins 19 secs

Tommy James and the Shondells are a rock band who have had thirteen Top 40 hits, including six in the Hot 100's top ten. Crimson and Clover was the bands second No.1 record (the other being Hanky Panky in July 1966) and sold an estimated 5 million copies, although the RIAA did not award a gold record so the 5 million sales number is not officially acknowledged. The song was recorded in late 1968 and is notable as being one of the earliest songs recorded on 16-track equipment.

1969: TOP FILMS

1. **Butch Cassidy And The Sundance Kid** - *20th Century Fox*
2. **Midnight Cowboy** - *United Artists*
3. **Easy Rider** - *Columbia*
4. **Hello, Dolly!** - *20th Century Fox*
5. **Bob & Carol & Ted & Alice** - *Columbia*

OSCARS

Best Picture: Midnight Cowboy
Most Nominations: Anne Of The Thousand Days (10)
Most Wins: Butch Cassidy And The Sundance Kid (4)

Best Director: John Schlesinger - *Midnight Cowboy*

Best Actor: John Wayne - *True Grit*
Best Actress: Maggie Smith - *The Prime Of Miss Jean Brodie*
Best Supporting Actor: Gig Young - *They Shoot Horses, Don't They?*
Best Supporting Actress: Goldie Hawn - *Cactus Flower*

The 42nd Academy Awards were presented on April 7, 1970.

Butch Cassidy and the Sundance Kid

Directed by: George Roy Hill - Runtime: 1 hour 50 minutes

Butch Cassidy and The Sundance Kid are the leaders of a band of outlaws in Wyoming in the early 1900s. After a train robbery goes wrong they find themselves on the run with a posse hard on their heels. Their solution - escape to Bolivia.

STARRING

Paul Newman
Born: January 26, 1925
Died: September 26, 2008

Character:
Butch Cassidy

Paul Leonard Newman was an American actor, IndyCar driver, entrepreneur, activist, and philanthropist. He won numerous acting awards including an Oscar for his role in the 1986 film The Color Of Money. He starred in many other classic films including The Hustler (1961), Cool Hand Luke (1967) and The Sting (1973). Newman co-founded food company Newman's Own which has so far donated over US$485 million to charity.

Robert Redford
Born: August 18, 1936

Character:
The Sundance Kid

Actor, director, producer, businessman, environmentalist, philanthropist and the founder of the Sundance Film Festival. He made his film debut in 1962 but it was his role in Butch Cassidy And The Sundance Kid which made him a major star. He has received two Academy Awards: one in 1981 for directing Ordinary People and one for Lifetime Achievement in 2002. In 2016 Redford was honored with the Presidential Medal of Freedom.

Katharine Ross
Born: January 29, 1940

Character:
Etta Place

Katharine Juliet Ross is an American film and stage actress. She had starring roles in three of the most popular films of the 1960s and 1970s: as Elaine Robinson in The Graduate (1967), for which she received a nomination for the Academy Award for Best Supporting Actress; as Etta Place in Butch Cassidy And The Sundance Kid, for which she won a BAFTA Award for Best Actress; and as Joanna Eberhart in The Stepford Wives (1975).

TRIVIA

Goofs | In the opening sequence, when Sundance shoots the gun belt off the card player, the film has been cut to make the quick draw appear faster - you can see Butch Cassidy's image jump across the screen in the background.

The foot-pegs through the front axle of the bicycle that Etta uses disappear during Butch Cassidy's stunt performance and reappear afterwards.

Interesting Facts | With nine wins the film currently holds the record for the most British Academy Awards (BAFTAs).

CONTINUED

Interesting Facts

The real Butch Cassidy, whose name was actually Robert Leroy Parker, got his nickname because he once worked in a butcher's shop. The Sundance Kid, real name Harry Alonzo Longabaugh, got his nickname because he once was arrested in the Wyoming town of Sundance.

Robert Redford wanted to do all of his own stunts. Paul Newman was especially upset about Redford's desire to jump onto the train roof and run along the tops of the cars as it moved. Redford said Newman told him, "I don't want any heroics around here. I don't want to lose a co-star."

Katharine Ross enjoyed shooting the silent bicycle riding sequence best because it was handled by the film crew's Second Unit rather than the director. She said, "Any day away from George Roy Hill was a good one".

The bull's name in the film is Bill. He was flown in from Los Angeles for the bicycle scene, which was shot in Utah. In order to make Bill charge a substance was sprayed on his testicles. Oddly he didn't seem to mind and endured it through several takes.

The Writers Guild of America ranked the screenplay number eleven on its list of the 101 Greatest Screenplays ever written.

Quotes

Butch Cassidy: Do you believe I'm broke already?
Etta Place: Why is there never any money, Butch?
Butch Cassidy: Well, I swear, Etta, I don't know. I've been working like a dog all my life and I can't get a penny ahead.
Etta Place: Sundance says it's because you're a soft touch, and always taking expensive vacations, and buying drinks for everyone, and you're a rotten gambler.
Butch Cassidy: Well that might have something to do with it.

Butch Cassidy: Kid, there's something I ought to tell you. I never shot anybody before.
Sundance Kid: One hell of a time to tell me!

MIDNIGHT COWBOY

Directed by: John Schlesinger - Runtime: 1 hour 53 minutes

Naive hustler Joe Buck travels from Texas to New York City to seek personal fortune and finds a new friend in crook Enrico Salvatore 'Ratso' Rizzo.

STARRING

Dustin Hoffman
Born: August 8, 1937

Character:
Ratso Rizzo

Actor and director with a career in film, television and theatre since 1960. He has been known for his versatile portrayals of antiheroes and vulnerable characters. Hoffman has been nominated for seven Academy Awards, winning twice for Best Actor in Kramer vs. Kramer (1979), and Rain Man (1988). He has also won six Golden Globes (including an honorary one) and four BAFTAs.

Jon Voight
Born: December 29, 1938

Character:
Joe Buck

Jonathan Vincent Voight is an actor who first came to prominence in Midnight Cowboy with his Oscar nominated performance as would-be gigolo Joe Buck. During the 1970s he became a Hollywood star with his portrayals of a businessman mixed up with murder in Deliverance (1972); a paraplegic Vietnam veteran in Coming Home (1978), for which he won an Academy Award for Best Actor; and a penniless ex-boxing champion in the remake of The Champ (1979).

Sylvia Miles
Born: September 9, 1924

Character:
Cass

Film, stage, and television actress whose career started in 1960 playing the role of Sadie in the film Murder, Inc. She has been nominated twice for the Academy Award for Best Supporting Actress for her performances as an aging Park Avenue kept-woman in Midnight Cowboy, despite only appearing on-screen for about six minutes, and for her slightly larger role (eight minutes) as Jessie Halstead Florian in Farewell, My Lovely (1975).

TRIVIA

Goofs	After Joe Buck's encounter with Towny he and Ratso board the bus to Miami. The bus then enters the south tube of the Lincoln Tunnel which only carries eastbound traffic into New York.
	A ceilingless set and lighting equipment can be briefly seen in several shots in Cass' bedroom.
Interesting Facts	Jon Voight was paid the Screen Actors Guild minimum wage for his portrayal of Joe Buck, a concession he willingly made to obtain the part.

CONTINUED

Interesting Facts

Before Dustin Hoffman auditioned for this film he knew that his all-American image could easily cost him the job. To prove he could do it he asked the auditioning film executive to meet him on a street corner in Manhattan, and in the meantime, dressed himself in filthy rags. The executive arrived at the appointed corner and waited, barely noticing Hoffman dressed as a "beggar" less than ten feet away accosting people for spare change. Eventually Hoffman walked up to him and revealed his true identity.

On the occasion of the film's 25th anniversary in 1994, Hoffman revealed on Larry King Live that when the movie was first previewed the audience started to leave in droves during gay encounter scene between Jon Voight and Bob Balaban.

The film was banned in Ireland by the Irish Film Censorship Board in September 1969. It did eventually receive a theatrical release in Ireland in 1971 when it was passed with an 18 certificate by the Irish Film Appeals Board.

Dustin Hoffman spent a considerable amount of time in the New York City slums observing tramps and studying their physical movements and behavior.

Warren Beatty was interested in playing Joe Buck but John Schlesinger thought he was too famous to be believable as a naive street hustler.

Quotes

Ratso Rizzo: You know, in my own place, my name ain't Ratso. I mean, it just so happens that in my own place my name is Enrico Salvatore Rizzo.
Joe Buck: Well, I can't say all that.
Ratso Rizzo: Rico, then.

Ratso Rizzo: Come on man, don't hit me. Come on, man. Come on, I'm a cripple!
Joe Buck: I ain't gonna hit you!
Ratso Rizzo: Come on...
Joe Buck: I'm gonna STRANGLE you to death!

Ratso Rizzo: I'm walking here! I'm walking here!

EASY RIDER

Directed by: Dennis Hopper - Runtime: 1 hour 35 minutes

Two bikers head from L.A to New Orleans and along the way meet a man who bridges a counter-culture gap they are unaware of.

STARRING

Peter Fonda
Born: February 23, 1940

Character:
Wyatt

Actor who made his professional stage debut on Broadway in 1961 in Blood, Sweat And Stanley Poole, for which he received rave reviews from the New York Critics, won the Daniel Blum Theater World Award and the New York Critics Circle Award for Best New Actor. He has been nominated twice for an Academy Award, once for Best Original Screenplay for Easy Rider (1969), and again for Best Actor in Ulee's Gold (1997).

Dennis Hopper
Born: May 17, 1936
Died: May 29, 2010

Characters:
Billy

Actor, director, writer, film editor, photographer and artist. He made his first television appearance in 1954 and soon after appeared alongside James Dean in the film Rebel Without A Cause (1955). In the next ten years he made a name in television and by the end of the 1960s had appeared in several films. Hopper also began a prolific and acclaimed photography career in the 1960s, and in 1969 also made his directorial film debut with Easy Rider.

Jack Nicholson
Born: April 22, 1937

Character:
George Hanson

John Joseph Nicholson is an actor and filmmaker who has performed for over sixty years. His 12 Academy Award nominations make him the most nominated male actor in the Academy's history and he is one of only three male actors to win three Oscars; he won an Academy Award for Best Actor for his roles in One Flew Over The Cuckoo's Nest (1975) and for As Good As It Gets (1997), and for Best Supporting Actor in Terms Of Endearment (1983).

TRIVIA

Goofs | In one of the riding across the bridge montage scenes you can see the camera man filming from the trunk of a car in the reflection of Wyatt's sunglasses.

The scene just before Wyatt throws away his watch is a mirror image. The bike appears to be leaning to the right on the kickstand (instead of the left) and his jacket has stripes down the right side but in the rest of the movie they're down the left side.

Interesting Facts | Peter Fonda, Dennis Hopper and Jack Nicholson were actually smoking marijuana on camera. LSD, however, was not actually used during the acid scene.

CONTINUED

Interesting Facts Dennis Hopper and Peter Fonda did not write a full script for the movie and made most of it up as they went along. They didn't hire a crew but instead picked up hippies at communes across the country and used friends and passers-by to hold the cameras.

Easy Rider was one of the first films to make extensive use of previously released musical tracks rather than a specially written film score. This is common with films now but was quite unusual at the time.

Some of the weird lighting effects in the LSD scene came about because a can of film was accidentally exposed when it was opened before being developed.

According to Peter Fonda four police bikes were customized for the film. One was burned during filming and the other three were stolen before filming was completed.

Karen Black described the shoot as "insane". According to Jack Nicholson, "Everyone wanted to kill one another and put one another in institutions".

Quotes **Wyatt:** *[reading inscription]* If god did not exist it would be necessary to invent him.
Billy: That's a humdinger!

George Hanson: *[Drinking his Jim Beam]* Here's the first of the day fellas! To old D.H. Lawrence.
[He starts flapping one arm like a chicken]
George Hanson: Neh! Neh! Neh! Fuh! Fuh! Fuh! Indians.

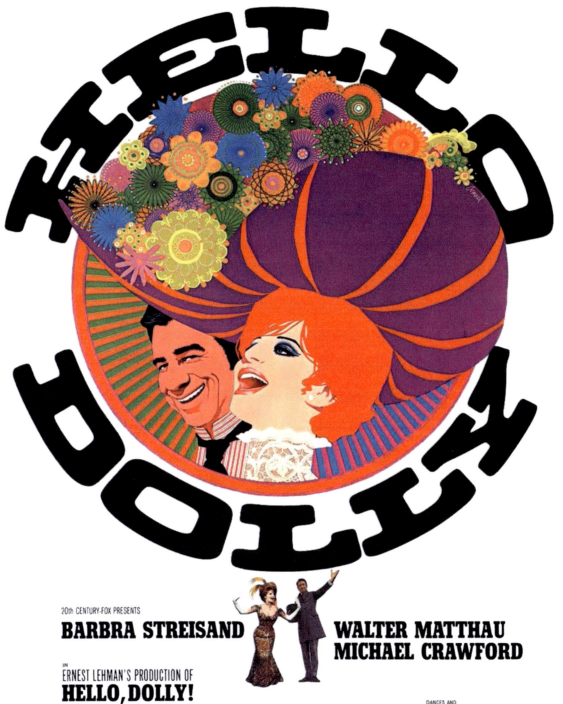

Directed by: Gene Kelly - Runtime: 2 hours 26 minutes

In 1890s New York City the bold and enchanting widow Dolly Levi is a socialite-turned-matchmaker. The film follows her exploits as she travels to Yonkers to find a match for the miserly 'well-known unmarried half-a-millionaire' Horace Vandergelder.

STARRING

Barbra Streisand
Born: April 24, 1942

Character:
Dolly Levi

Singer, songwriter, actress and filmmaker. During a career spanning six decades she has become an icon in multiple fields of entertainment winning two Academy Awards - for Funny Girl (1968) and A Star Is Born (1976) - ten Grammys, five Emmys, a Special Tony Award, an American Film Institute Award, a Kennedy Center Honors prize, four Peabody Awards and nine Golden Globes. In 2015 she was awarded the Presidential Medal of Freedom by Barack Obama.

Walter Matthau
Born: October 1, 1920
Died: July 1, 2000

Character:
Horace Vandergelder

Actor and comedian best known for his role as Oscar Madison in The Odd Couple and his frequent collaborations with Odd Couple co-star Jack Lemmon (particularly in the 1990's with Grumpy Old Men and its sequel Grumpier Old Men). Matthau won the Academy Award for Best Supporting Actor for his performance in the Billy Wilder film The Fortune Cookie (1966), and was also the winner of two BAFTA's, a Golden Globe and two Tony awards.

Michael Crawford
Born: January 19, 1942

Character:
Cornelius Hackl

Actor, comedian, singer, voice artist and philanthropist born Michael Patrick Smith. Crawford has received international critical acclaim and won numerous awards during his career, which has included many film and television performances as well as stagework on both London's West End and on Broadway in New York City. He is probably best known for playing the character Frank Spencer in the 1970s British sitcom Some Mothers Do 'Ave 'Em and for originating the title role in The Phantom Of The Opera.

TRIVIA

Goofs	Although the film is set in 1890 modern electrical power transformers are visible on the utility poles in the Yonkers scenes.
	The red-carpeted staircase at the Harmonia Gardens restaurant has brass carpet rods on each stair during all of the scenes prior to the arrival of Dolly Levi. When she arrives and they sing 'Hello, Dolly!' the carpet rods are gone.
Interesting Facts	Gene Kelly fought to keep Michael Crawford's singing voice, which the producers wanted to dub.

CONTINUED

Interesting Facts Barbra Streisand and Walter Matthau fought bitterly during filming. He disliked her so intensely that he refused to be around her unless the script required it. He is famously quoted as telling Streisand that she "had no more talent than a butterfly's fart".

On a break from filming, Walter Matthau and Michael Crawford visited a nearby racetrack and saw a horse named Hello Dolly. Matthau refused to place a bet on it because it reminded him of Barbra Streisand. Crawford placed a bet on the horse. It won the race and Matthau refused to speak to Crawford for the rest of the shoot unless absolutely necessary.

This was the very first film released on home video (VHS and Betamax) in the U.S. It was released in fall 1977 by the Magnetic Video Corporation, the first of the 50 original films it licensed from Fox. Its catalog number was CL-1001.

In the Harmonia Gardens, the back wall behind the hat-check girl is the wall from the ballroom of the Von Trapps Villa in The Sound of Music (1965).

Hello, Dolly! was the most expensive musical ever produced at the time of the film's release.

Quotes **Dolly Levi:** Money, pardon the expression, is like manure. It's not worth a thing unless it's spread around, encouraging young things to grow.

Horace Vandergelder: Eighty percent of the people in the world are fools and the rest of us are in danger of contamination.

BOB & CAROL & TED & ALICE

consider the possibilities

COLUMBIA PICTURES presents
A FRANKOVICH PRODUCTION

NATALIE WOOD   **ROBERT CULP**

BOB & CAROL & TED & ALICE

ELLIOTT GOULD   **DYAN CANNON**

Directed by: Paul Mazursky - Runtime: 1 hour 45 minutes

After a weekend of emotional honesty at an Esalen-style retreat, Los Angeles sophisticates Bob and Carol Sanders return home determined to embrace complete openness. The couple then proceed share their enthusiasm and excitement over their new-found philosophy with their more conservative friends Ted and Alice Henderson.

STARRING

Natalie Wood
Born: July 20, 1938
Died: November 29, 1981

Character:
Carol Sanders

Russian-American actress born Natalia Nikolaevna Zakharenko. Wood began her career in film as a child and became a successful Hollywood star as a young adult, receiving three Academy Award nominations before she turned 25 years old. Notable films include Miracle On 34th Street (1947), Rebel Without A Cause (1955), West Side Story (1961), Gypsy (1962), Splendor In The Grass (1961) and Love With The Proper Stranger (1963).

Robert Culp
Born: August 16, 1930
Died: March 24, 2010

Character:
Bob Sanders

An actor, screenwriter, voice actor, and director, widely known for his work in television in a career spanning more than 50 years. Culp earned an international reputation for his role as Kelly Robinson on I Spy (1965-1968) and worked as an actor in many theatrical films, beginning with three in 1963; PT 109, The Raiders, and Sunday In New York. The 1980s brought him back to television starring in The Greatest American Hero, and Everybody Loves Raymond.

Elliott Gould
Born: August 29, 1938

Characters:
Ted Henderson

Actor born Elliott Goldstein who began acting in Hollywood films during the 1960s. Gould is perhaps best known for his significant leading roles in Robert Altman films; starring in M*A*S*H (1970), The Long Goodbye (1973), and California Split (1974). More recently he has gained recognition for his recurring supporting roles as Jack Geller on Friends (1994-2004), as Reuben Tishkoff in the Ocean's Trilogy (2001-2007), and as Ezra Goldman in Ray Donovan (2013-2015).

TRIVIA

Goofs | In the restaurant kitchen Carol takes hold of the waiter's left hand but in the next shot she is holding his right hand.

The camera crew's reflections are visible during the opening helicopter shots.

Interesting Facts | Natalie Wood decided to gamble her standard fee on a percentage of the gross. This earned her $3 million and averted her making the same mistake she did when she declined a similar offer with West Side Story (1961).

CONTINUED

Interesting Facts This was Natalie Wood's first film since starring in Penelope (1966). She would not star in another movie for four years when she would co-star in The Affair (1973) with her first husband Robert Wagner (with whom she had recently remarried).

Donald F. Muhich who played Alice Henderson's therapist was director Paul Mazursky's real-life therapist. He later appeared in three other Mazursky films.

Actors who turned down roles in the film included Warren Beatty, Robert Redford, Steve McQueen, Tuesday Weld, Jane Fonda and Faye Dunaway.

Quotes **Alice Henderson:** You know how children are, they're very curious. He wanted to know why I had a tee-tee...
Psychiatrist: Pardon me? I don't know what a tee-tee is.
Alice Henderson: A vagina.
Psychiatrist: Oh, it's a pet expression of yours.
Alice Henderson: Yes, you know words: tee-tee, tinkle, po-po, wee-wee, kee-kee, poo-poo.
Psychiatrist: I had never heard tee-tee before.
Alice Henderson: What expression do you use with your children?
Psychiatrist: Vagina.

Sporting Winners

Tom Seaver - Major League Baseball

 Associated Press - Male Athlete of the Year

George Thomas Seaver
Born: November 17, 1944 in Fresno, California
MLB debut: April 13, 1967 for the New York Mets
Last MLB appearance: September 19, 1986 for the Boston Red Sox

Tom Seaver, nicknamed Tom Terrific and The Franchise, is a retired Major League Baseball pitcher. He pitched from 1967 to 1986 for four teams, but is noted primarily for his time with the New York Mets and especially for his important role in the team's 1969 World Championship. He won the National League Rookie of the Year Award in 1967 and he has received three NL Cy Young Awards as the league's best pitcher. Seaver is the Mets' all-time leader in wins and he is considered by many baseball experts to be one of the best starting pitchers in the history of baseball.

Career Highlights / Awards:

All-Star	1967-1973, 1975-1978, 1981
World Series Champion	1969
NL Cy Young Award	1969, 1973, 1975
NL Rookie Of The Year	1967
NL Wins Leader	1969, 1975, 1981
NL ERA Leader	1970, 1971, 1973
NL Strikeout Leader	1970, 1971, 1973, 1975, 1976

Win-loss record 311-205, Earned run average 2.86, Strikeouts 3,640

In 1992 Seaver was inducted into the National Baseball Hall of Fame by the highest percentage of votes ever recorded at the time (425 of 430 - 98.84%; subsequently surpassed in 2016 by Ken Griffey Jr. with 437 of 440 - 99.32%).

Debbie Meyer - Swimming

Associated Press - Female Athlete of the Year

Deborah Elizabeth Meyer
Born: August 14, 1952 in Annapolis, Maryland

Debbie Meyer, also known by her married name Deborah Weber, is a former competition swimmer, a three-time Olympic champion and a former world record-holder in four events; Meyer won her 3 Olympic medals whilst she was still a 16-year-old student at Rio Americano High School in Sacramento, California. During her career she also broke 24 American records and won 19 Amateur Athletic Union (AAU) national championships.

Medals:

Year	Competition	Location	Event	Medal
1968	Olympic Games	Mexico City	200m Freestyle	Gold
			400m Freestyle	Gold
			800m Freestyle	Gold

Year	Competition	Location	Event	Medal
1967	Pan American Games	Winnipeg	400m Freestyle	Gold
			800m Freestyle	Gold

In 1968 Meyer won the James E. Sullivan Award and in 1969 she was named Associated Press Female Athlete of the Year. She was also named Swimming World's World Swimmer of the Year in 1967, 1968 and 1969. Meyer retired from swimming in 1972 and was inducted into the International Swimming Hall of Fame in 1977 and the U.S. Olympic Hall of Fame in 1986.

GOLF

THE MASTERS - GEORGE ARCHER

The Masters Tournament is the first of the majors to be played each year and unlike the other major championships it is played at the same location, Augusta National Golf Club, Georgia. This was the 33rd Masters Tournament and was held April 10-13. George Archer won his only major championship, one stroke ahead of runners-up Billy Casper, George Knudson and Tom Weiskopf, to take home the $20,000 winner's share of the prize fund.

U.S. OPEN - ORVILLE MOODY

The 1969 U.S. Open Championship (established in 1895) was held June 12-15 at the Cypress Creek Course of Champions Golf Club in Houston, Texas. Orville Moody won his only PGA Tour title, one stroke ahead of runners-up Deane Beman, Bob Rosburg and Al Geiberger; 35 year old Moody's only other career top-10 finish in a major came two months later at the PGA Championship. The total prize fund for the U.S. Open was $205,300 with Moody taking home $30,000.

PGA CHAMPIONSHIP - RAYMOND FLOYD

The 1969 and 51st PGA Championship was played August 14-17 at the South Course of NCR Country Club in Kettering, Ohio, a suburb south of Dayton. Raymond Floyd, age 26, won the first of his four major titles, one stroke ahead of runner-up Gary Player. The total prize fund was $175,000 of which $35,000 went to the champion Floyd.

Oliver Moody

George Archer

Raymond Floyd

WORLD SERIES - NEW YORK METS

4 - 1

New York Mets **Baltimore Orioles**

Total attendance: 272,378 - Average attendance: 54,476
Winning player's share: $18,338 - Losing player's share: $14,904

The World Series is the annual championship series of Major League Baseball played since 1903 between the American League and the National League champion teams. It is determined through a best-of-seven playoff.

The 1969 World Series saw the National League champions, the New York Mets, beating the American League champions, the Baltimore Orioles, by four games to one. The Mets became the first expansion team to win a division title, a pennant, and the World Series, winning in their eighth year of existence.

New York Mets players celebrate winning game 5 and the 1969 World Series.

	Date	Score			Location	Time	Att.
1	Oct 11	Mets	1-4	**Orioles**	Memorial Stadium	2:13	50,429
2	Oct 12	**Mets**	2-1	Orioles	Memorial Stadium	2:20	50,850
3	Oct 14	Orioles	0-5	**Mets**	Shea Stadium	2:23	56,335
4	Oct 15	Orioles	1-2	**Mets**	Shea Stadium	2:33	57,367
5	Oct 16	Orioles	3-5	**Mets**	Shea Stadium	2:14	57,397

Horse Racing

Arts and Letters takes the Belmont Stakes from second place Majestic Prince.

Arts and Letters (April 1, 1966 - October 16, 1998) was an American Hall of Fame Champion Thoroughbred racehorse who was owned and bred by sportsman and noted philanthropist Paul Mellon, and trained by future Hall of Famer Elliott Burch. Arts and Letters was the leading American colt of his generation and was voted United States Horse of the Year in 1969. In the 1969 Classic races he came second in both the Kentucky Derby and Preakness stakes, before winning the Belmont Stakes. During his racing career he ran in a total of 23 races of which he won 11; his total earnings were $632,404.

Kentucky Derby - Majestic Prince

The Kentucky Derby is held annually at Churchill Downs in Louisville, Kentucky on the first Saturday in May. The race is a Grade 1 stakes race for three-year-olds and is one and a quarter miles in length.

Preakness Stakes - Majestic Prince

The Preakness Stakes is held on the third Saturday in May each year at Pimlico Race Course in Baltimore, Maryland. It is a Grade 1 race run over a distance of 9.5 furlongs (1 3/16 miles) on dirt.

Belmont Stakes - Arts and Letters

The Belmont Stakes is Grade 1 race held every June at Belmont Park in Elmont, New York. It is 1.5 miles in length and open to three-year-old thoroughbreds. It takes place on a Saturday between June 5 and June 11.

American Football

Super Bowl IV

7 - 23

Minnesota Vikings
NFL

Kansas City Chiefs
AFL

Played: January 11, 1970 at the Tulane Stadium in New Orleans, Louisiana
MVP: Len Dawson, Quarterback (Kansas City Chiefs)
Referee: John McDonough - Attendance: 80,562

American Football League

Division	Team	P	W	L	T	PCT	PF	PA
Eastern Division	New York Jets	14	10	4	0	.714	353	269
Western Division	Oakland Raiders	14	12	1	1	.923	377	242

The 1969 American Football League season was the tenth and final regular season of the American Football League before AFL-NFL Merger. The season ended when The Chiefs defeated the Oakland Raiders in the final AFL Championship Game on January 4, 1970 at the Oakland-Alameda County Coliseum.

National Football League

Division	Team	P	W	L	T	PCT	PF	PA
Capitol (Eastern)	Dallas Cowboys	14	11	2	1	.846	369	223
Century (Eastern)	Cleveland Browns	14	10	3	1	.769	351	300
Coastal (Western)	Los Angeles Rams	14	11	3	0	.786	320	243
Central (Western)	Minnesota Vikings	14	12	2	0	.857	379	133

The 1969 NFL season was the 50th regular season of the National Football League and the last one before the AFL-NFL Merger. The season ended when the Minnesota Vikings defeated the Cleveland Browns in the NFL championship game on January 4, 1970 at the Metropolitan Stadium in Bloomington, Minnesota. *Fun Fact: 1969 saw the The Philadelphia Eagles become the first NFL team to play its home games on artificial turf (installed at Franklin Field).*

NHL Finals - Stanley Cup

 4 - 0

Montreal Canadiens   **St. Louis Blues**

Series Summary:

	Date	Home Team	Result	Road Team
1	April 27	St. Louis Blues	1-3	**Montreal Canadiens**
2	April 29	St. Louis Blues	1-3	**Montreal Canadiens**
3	May 1	**Montreal Canadiens**	4-0	St. Louis Blues
4	May 4	**Montreal Canadiens**	2-1	St. Louis Blues

The 1969 Stanley Cup Finals saw the Canadiens take the series in four straight games in a repeat of the previous years' final. The Stanley Cup MVP was Serge Savard (Canadiens).

Basketball - NBA Finals

 4 - 3

Boston Celtics   **Los Angeles Lakers**

Series Summary:

	Date	Home Team	Result	Road Team
1	April 23	**Los Angeles Lakers**	120-118	Boston Celtics
2	April 25	**Los Angeles Lakers**	118-112	Boston Celtics
3	April 27	**Boston Celtics**	111-105	Los Angeles Lakers
4	April 29	**Boston Celtics**	89-88	Los Angeles Lakers
5	May 1	**Los Angeles Lakers**	117-104	Boston Celtics
6	May 3	**Boston Celtics**	99-90	Los Angeles Lakers
7	May 5	Los Angeles Lakers	106-108	**Boston Celtics**

The 1969 NBA World Championship Series saw the Celtics defeat the Lakers in seven games. The Lakers were heavily favored and their loss is considered one of the great upsets in NBA history. *Fun Fact: This was the first year a Finals MVP award was given and remains the only time in NBA Finals history that the MVP was awarded to a player on the losing team (Jerry West).*

INDIANAPOLIS 500 - MARIO ANDRETTI

Mario Andretti in his Indy 500 winning Brawner Hawk.

The 53rd International 500-Mile Sweepstakes Race was held at the Indianapolis Motor Speedway on Friday, May 30, 1969, and was won by Mario Andretti in front of an estimated crowd of 275,000 spectators. Andretti led for 116 laps total and finished with a time of 3h 11m 14s; it was the fastest run race up to that date and broke the previous record by nearly five minutes

Mario Gabriele Andretti (b. February 28, 1940) is one of the most successful Americans in the history of motor sport and is one of only two drivers to have won races in Formula One, IndyCar, World Sportscar Championship and NASCAR (the other being Dan Gurney). In 2000 the Associated Press and RACER magazine named him Driver of the Century.

BOSTON MARATHON
YOSHIAKI UNETANI

The Boston Marathon is the oldest annual marathon in the world and dates back to 1897. It is always held on Patriots' Day, the third Monday of April, and was inspired by the success of the first marathon competition at the 1896 Summer Olympics.

Race Result:

Pos.	Competitor	Country	Time
1.	**Yoshiaki Unetani**	**Japan**	**2:13:49**
2.	Pablo Garrido	Mexico	2:17:30
3.	Alfredo Penaloza	Mexico	2:19:56

Tennis - U.S. Open

Margaret Court and Rod Laver with their U.S. Open trophies.

Men's Singles Champion - Rod Laver - Australia
Ladies Singles Champion - Margaret Court - Australia

The 1969 U.S. Open (formerly known as U.S. National Championships) took place on the outdoor grass courts at the West Side Tennis Club, Forest Hills in New York. It was the 89th staging of the tournament and it ran from August 29 to September 8.

Men's Singles Final

Country	Player	Set 1	Set 2	Set 3	Set 4
Australia	Rod Laver	7	6	6	6
Australia	Tony Roche	9	1	2	2

Women's Singles Final

Country	Player	Set 1	Set 2
Australia	Margaret Court	6	6
United States	Nancy Richey	2	2

Men's Doubles Final

Country	Players	Set 1	Set 2	Set 3	Set 4
Australia	Ken Rosewall / Fred Stolle	2	7	13	6
United States	Charlie Pasarell / Dennis Ralston	6	5	11	3

Women's Doubles Final

Country	Players	Set 1	Set 2	Set 3
France / United States	Françoise Dürr / Darlene Hard	0	6	6
Australia / United Kingdom	Margaret Court / Virginia Wade	6	4	4

Mixed Doubles Final

Country	Players	Set 1	Set 2
Australia / United States	Margaret Court / Marty Riessen	7	6
France / United States	Françoise Dürr / Dennis Ralston	5	3

The Cost Of Living

Comparison Chart

	1969 Price	1969 (+ Inflation)	2018 Price	% Change
Annual Income	$2,900	$19,947	$57,817	+189.8%
House	$27,800	$191,221	$295,000	+54.3%
Car	$3,500	$24,075	$33,560	+39.4%
Gallon Of Gasoline	39¢	$2.68	$2.43	-9.3%
Gallon Of Milk	45¢	$3.10	$4.42	+42.6%
DC Comic Book	12¢	83¢	$3.99	+380.7%

GROCERIES

Kraft Parkay Margarine (1lb ctn.)	25¢
Lucerne Evaporated Milk (7x 14½oz cans)	$1
June Clarks Small Eggs (3 dozen)	$1
Imperial Pure Cane Sugar (10lb bag)	89¢
Foremost Cottage Cheese (1lb ctn.)	29¢
Kraft Cheese (12oz pkg.)	67¢
Hungry Jack Biscuits (2x 9½oz cans)	43¢
Sunshine Crackers (1lb)	39¢
Sara Lee Caramel Pecan Cake (11oz pkg.)	85¢
Mrs Wright's Assorted Cake Mix (18½oz pkg.)	25¢
Pillsbury Extra Light Pancake Mix (2lb box)	41¢
Safeway Corn Flakes (12oz pkg.)	29¢
Sunkist Valencia Oranges (per lb)	15¢
Washington State Red Apples (per lb)	19¢
Vine Ripe Tomatoes (per lb)	19¢
Crispy Green California Lettuce (per lb)	10¢
Texas Cabbage (per lb)	7¢
Bel-Air Green Peas (10oz pkg.)	16¢
U.S. No.1 Russett Potatoes (10lb bag)	79¢
U.S. No.1 Crispy Yellow Onions (per lb)	5¢
T-Bone Steak (per lb)	$1.29
USDA Heavy Beef Round Steak (per lb)	89¢
Pork Chops (per lb)	79¢
Boneless Ham (per lb)	$1.39
Armour's Sliced Bacon (1lb pkg.)	79¢
Tennessee Farm Sausages (2lb pkg.)	$1.59
Fryers (per lb)	29¢
Brilliant Frozen Cooked Shrimp (10oz pkg.)	95¢
Fresh Louisiana Oysters (12oz jar)	89¢
Banquet Frozen Dinners (11oz)	39¢
Bel-Air Cheese Pizza (16oz pkg.)	65¢
Del Monte Fruit Cocktail (303 can)	19¢
Del Monte Catsup (14oz bottle)	19¢
Heinz Worchester Sauce (5oz bottle)	39¢
Maxwell House Coffee (1lb)	69¢
Tenderleaf Instant Tea (2oz jar)	79¢
Coca-Cola (3x 6 bottle cartons)	$1
Bel-Air Orange Juice (5x 6oz cans)	$1
Santa Rosa Pineapple Juice (46oz can)	25¢
Truly Fine Hair Spray (13oz aerosol)	49¢
Head & Shoulders Shampoo (regular size)	69¢
Max Factor Hand Cream	$1.95
Gillett Soft & Dry Anti-Perspirant	98¢
Vicks Vapo Rub	79¢
Brocode Toilet Tissue (3x 4 rolls)	$1
Purex Liquid Bleach (½ gallon jug)	29¢
Pooch Dog Food (12x 15½oz cans)	$1
Nine Lives Cat Food (6½oz can)	10¢

CLOTHES

Women's Clothing

J.M. Dyer White Popcorn Wool Coat	$98.50
Woolworth Suburban Coat	$22
Beall's All-Weather Coat	$11.88
Crimped Nylon Scarf (x4)	$1
Dacron Polyester Dress	$10.88
Levines Bonded Knit Fall Dress	$8
K. Wolens Sweater	$3.99 - $12.95
Beall's Nylon Capri Pants	$5.88
Lacy Nylon Peignor Set	$3.99
Nylon Briefs (x2)	88¢
Petite Belle Seamless Nylons (x3)	$1
Levines Vinyl Knee Stretch Boots	$5.99
Cooper's Life Stride Wet Look Shoes	$18
Miss Jennifer Plain Pumps	$8.88
Woolworth Ballerina Slippers	57¢

Full-fashioned, washable
BULKY CARDIGAN

Our own Primstyle® acrylic knit with cable stitch front, ribbed accents. Perfect over skirts, pants, shorts. Many colors. S-M-L.

$6.99

Medium weight...fancy front
ACRYLIC CARDIGANS

Cable knits in three pretty designs. All with crew necks. Washable. Here in white and assorted pastel colors. Misses' 34 to 40.

$4.99

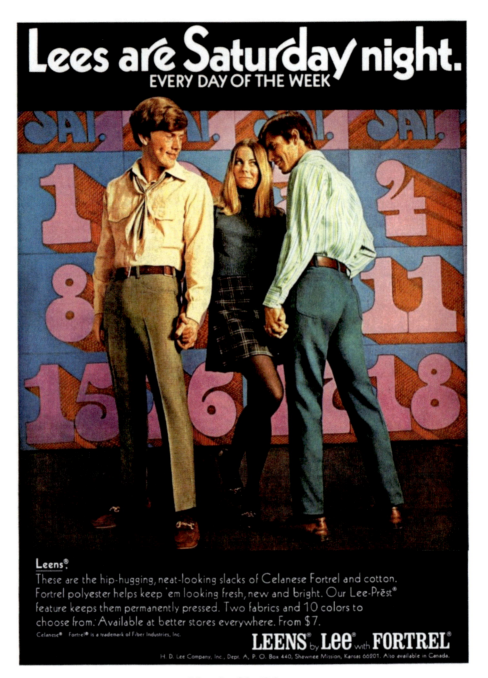

Men's Clothing

Beall's All-Weather Coat	$16.88
P. Samuels Sports Coat	from $30
Harris & Jacobs Palm Beach Fall Suit	$89.95
Woolworth Fisherman Knit Turtleneck	$9.99
Beall's Sweater	$8.88
Levines Dress Shirt (x3)	$10
Easy-Care Flared Slacks	$5
Dickie Khaki No-Iron Pants (x2)	$9
K. Wolens Pajamas	$3.49
Portage Black Leather Shoes	$21.95
Woolworth Rugged Oxford Work Shoes	$7.99
Orlon Stretch Socks (pair)	$1

TOYS

20in Roadmaster Renegade Bicycle	$38.99
Hi-Rise Girls Bicycle	$34.88
Mighty Tonka 18½in Dump Truck	$5.97
Remco Rudy The Robot	$9.88
Talking Baby First Step Doll	$15.88
Tiny Baby Crawler 11in Doll	$2.97
Doll Stroller	$2.97
Hot Wheels Drag Race Action Set	$6.88
Deluxe Gun & Holster Set	$1.97
Ker-Plunk - Exciting New Skill Game	$3.27
Twister	$3.67
Spirograph	$3.27
Weaving Loom Set	99¢
Slinky Walking Spring Toy	77¢
Go-Go Steel String Guitar	$9.57
Toy Trumpet	77¢
Woolworth Basketball Basket & Backboard	$13.97
Miniature Pool Table	$1.99
Wilson Football & Kicking Tee	$2.99
Gibson's Doctor Or Nurse Kit	69¢
Color Tone See Thru Spinning Top	$1.88

New from Mattel. The fastest miniature cars you've ever seen. And look at these features!

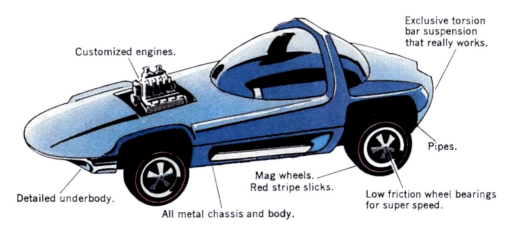

Choose from 16 new California custom styled Hot Wheels!

ELECTRICAL GOODS

Philco-Ford 23in Big-Screen Color TV	$439
General Electric Porta Color 180 TV	$359.95
Packard Bell 19in Portable B&W TV	$125
Hotpoint Double Oven	$348
Frigidaire Washer & Matching Dryer	$325
Frigidaire Fridge / Freezer	$340
Hotpoint Portable Dishwasher	$118.88
Portable Cassette Tape Recorder	$37.99
Hoover Vacuum Cleaner	$39.95
K. Wolens Queen Size Electric Blanket	$11.99
General Electric Coffee Maker	$10.88
Munsey Electric Oven Toaster	$4.44
Munsey Electric Corn Popper	$3.44
Hamilton Beach Mixette Portable Mixer	$8.88
Oster 10-Speed Blender	$28.88
West Bend Automatic Percolator	$11.88
Skilsaw Power Saw - 5½in Blade	$28.88
Oster Portable Professional Hair Dryer	$28.88
Imperial Electric Can Opener	$6.88
General Electric AM Clock Radio	$16.88
Sunbeam Electric Clock	$2.88

PERFORMANCE-GUARANTEED Big-Screen Color TV from Philco-Ford!

Philco® 23" *diag.* Color TV
- Philco 26,000-volt Cool Chassis
- Transistorized Solid State Signal System
- Philco MagiColor rare-earth phosphor picture tube— now 35% brighter than previous Philco picture tube
- Illuminated VHF/UHF channel indicators

*23" picture measured diagonally, 295 sq.in. picture

Outstanding value!

$439.00

PHILCO *Ford* The better idea people in Color TV

"Cutty Sark first... the rest nowhere"

1886.
CUTTY SARK
was the best.
She was number one.
Then, as now, you
had to be best to be first.
This distinguished Scotch
carries on her name
and her tradition.

America's No. 1 selling Scotch.

let's make it

Make yourself the greatest home bartender in town. Just send $3.50 to Early Times Glass Offer*—P. O. Box 1080, Louisville, Kentucky 40201. We'll send you a set of 6 Giant 15 oz. Early Times Jiggers. Or send $3.00, for a set of 8 Early Times 10½ oz. Highball Glasses. They're beautiful, so get both sets while they last. Do it now.
*offer valid only where legal

THE TRUE OLD-STYLE KENTUCKY BOURBON

NEW ...the alarm you only set once

WAKES YOU ON THE DAYS YOU WANT TO GET UP ...LETS YOU SLEEP ON THE OTHER DAYS!

Ever-Set*... the new General Electric alarm that lets you forget...because it remembers, automatically. Set it just once... wakes you morning after morning on the days you select. Never needs resetting! Can be set manually, too, for those days you want to get up at a different time. Has lighted dial for easy time telling in the dark, even across the room. 3½ in. high, 6 in. wide. Nutria or sandalwood color.

Only one of 140 great clocks from General Electric!
General Electric Company, Housewares Division, Bridgeport, Conn. 06602

GENERAL ELECTRIC

OTHER ITEMS

Chevrolet Corvette Stingray	$4,438
Pontiac Firebird Trans Am	$4,366
Jet Star 120 White Wall Tires 650x13	$19.99
7ft Pool Table	$89.88
Wingback Sleeper Sofa	$238
Remington 770ADL High Powered Rifle	$104.50
Marlin Model 30 Deer Rifle	$74.95
Woolworth 48in Professional Poker Table	$24.95
Polaroid 320 Land Camera	$47.77
Family Size 7-PC Dinette Set	$88
Bemco Comfapedic Mattress	$44
Swinger Portable Typewriter	$59.97
Baylor 2-Diamond 17-Jewel Ladies Watch	$39.95
Leading Brand Cigarettes (pack)	55¢

$100.00   **$100.00**

NOW IS THE TIME TO BUY
A BEAUTIFUL NEW HOME AT
QUALITY MOBILE HOMES
HWY 31 WEST
CORSICANA, TEXAS

Every home carefully selected to insure you many years for comfort and convenience with minimum upkeep. Build and equity in your future — own a Mobile Home with all new furnishings and precision factory controlled construction. Major brand appliances, heating, and plumbing fixtures. All prices are plainly marked in each home and include delivery and installation with in 50 miles with hook ups to your utilities — Here are a few examples!

12'	44'	1 b/r		3795.00
14'	50'	2 b/r		5200.00
14'	68'	2 b/r	2 full baths	9995.00

YOU WILL RECEIVE A GIFT CERTIFICATE FOR $100.00

Redeemable at WOOLWORTH STORES or Navarro Mall on any home purchased from now through December 20th.

BRING THIS AD

$100.00   **$100.00**

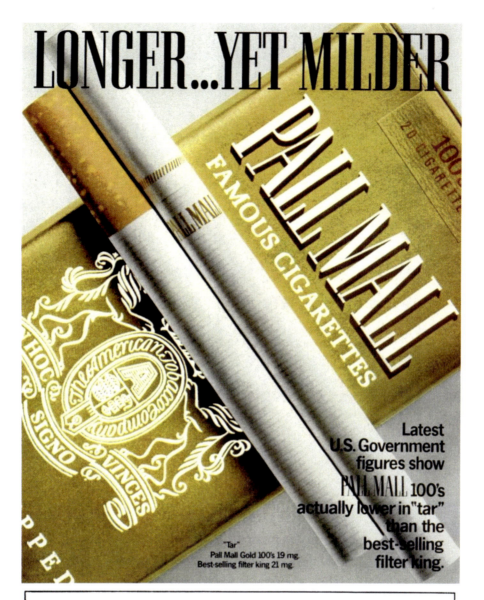

U.S. Coins

Official Circulated U.S. Coins		Years Produced
Half-Cent	½¢	1793 - 1857
Cent - Penny	1¢	1793 - Present
2-Cent (Bronze)	2¢	1864 - 1873
3-Cent (Nickle)	3¢	1865 - 1889
Trime (3-Cent Silver)	3¢	1851 - 1873
Half-Dime	5¢	1794 - 1873
Five Cent Nickel	5¢	1866 - Present
Dime	10¢	1796 - Present
20-Cent	20¢	1875 - 1878
Quarter	25¢	1796 - Present
Half Dollar	50¢	1794 - Present
Dollar Coin	$1	1794 - Present
Gold Dollar	$1	1849 - 1889
Quarter Eagle	$2.50	1796 - 1929
Three-Dollar Piece	$3	1854 - 1889
Four-Dollar Piece	$4	1879 - 1880
Half Eagle	$5	1795 - 1929
Gold Eagle	$10	1795 - 1933
Double Eagle	$20	1849 - 1933
Half Union	$50	1915

Big, strong and stylish. This is the way it's going to be.

Looks like a whole lot of designers got caught looking. Again.

While they were building their traditional "big cars," we were building the most luxurious Pontiac Bonneville ever. (So luxurious our upholstery has been attacked as unfair competition.)

We were also proving, once and for all, that being big is no excuse for being clumsy. With a new 455 V-8, firm suspension, Wide-Track stance.

Now, isn't that the way you want luxury to be? It is. At your Pontiac dealer's.

Pontiac's new Bonneville

(We take the fun of driving seriously.)

Comic Strips

'LIL ABNER

BARNEY GOOGLE AND SNUFFY SMITH

BLONDIE

BEETLE BAILEY

Made in the USA
Lexington, KY
10 September 2019